AMARANTH

An Ancient Grain
and
Exceptionally Nutritious Food

Robert L. Myers, Ph.D.

Harvest Road Publishing

Published 2018, First Printing
Harvest Road Publishing
Columbia, MO
Haley Myers, Editor

*Cover photo of grain amaranth and all other photos
in the book were taken by the author, unless otherwise
credited.*

DEDICATION

To the two mothers in my life:
My own terrific mom, who nurtured my love of
reading, driving me many times from our farm into
our rural town's library for books, and who shared
her love of flowers and gardening;
and
My wonderful mother-in-law, who loves books as
much as anyone I ever met, and is quite the fan of
amaranth, the "everlasting flower."

TABLE OF CONTENTS

The Rose and the Amaranth

A Rose and an Amaranth blossomed side by
side in a garden, and the Amaranth said to her
neighbor, "How I envy you your beauty and your
sweet scent! No wonder you are such a universal
favorite." But the Rose replied with a shade of
sadness in her voice, "Ah, my dear friend, I bloom
but for a time: my petals soon wither and fall, and
then I die. But your flowers never fade, even if they
are cut; for they are everlasting."

- Aesop

Illustration by Chelsea Wright

PREFACE

This book is about a fascinating food crop, grain amaranth, which was once a major crop in the Americas, was largely forgotten about after the Spanish conquests in the New World, and has now reemerged as a crop with great promise for the future. I first became aware of amaranth while doing my masters and Ph.D. studies in agronomy (crop and soil science) at University of Minnesota in the 1980s. As I describe in more detail in Chapter 1, the first time I saw a big farm field of amaranth was in 1987, though I had earlier seen a very small plot of it at the University of Minnesota St. Paul research field near campus, I think first in 1983. Dr. Bob Robinson, since passed away, was growing a little amaranth along with a wide variety of alternative crops, and helped spark my first interest in considering the benefits of diversifying farms with underutilized crops.

In the years since then, I've had periods of time where I did considerable research on amaranth, principally in the early 1990s and then for several years in the 2000s. For most of the last three decades, I've grown amaranth in my own garden and/or research fields. I've also worked on-farm with some producers growing amaranth. In the last several years, I've done a small breeding project with amaranth, to develop a couple of new grain amaranth varieties described in Chapter 5. Altogether I've done about 20 different research projects on amaranth over the years, and have had the opportunity to do more field trials studying how to grow grain amaranth than probably anyone else in the U.S., which isn't as impressive as it sounds, since only a handful of U.S. scientists have done much research on amaranth!

I will say that I learn something new about amaranth every year that I grow it, which now amounts to a total of 27 growing seasons of planting. About 15 of those years involved field research trials and some larger scale farm plantings, but I've also grown plots of it at home for most of those 27 years. Most of my personal experience with amaranth has been in Missouri, but I grew it in a home garden in Maryland when I lived there for a few years, and have visited amaranth fields and research plantings in several other states.

I've been fortunate to add to my knowledge about amaranth by visiting with other amaranth workers over the years, both from the U.S. and abroad, and reading the research done around the world on the crop. The collaborator I've worked with the most on amaranth is Alan Weber, a fellow Missourian, part-time farmer, and agricultural economist. Alan has been involved in a variety of amaranth projects with me, but has particularly helped me understand market opportunities with amaranth and how to think about the economics of alternative crops such as amaranth. He also worked with me in past years to assist farmers on how to grow amaranth and has grown grain amaranth on his own farm a few times over the years. I owe a great deal to him for his collaboration and support.

There are many amaranth workers I mention throughout the text of this book for their particular contributions, but I have to credit several people right up front in this book. First among peers in the amaranth community is David Brenner, who's been perhaps the most important person in the U.S. amaranth community over the last 30 years. He has done fundamentally important investigations into various types of amaranth in his role as the amaranth curator with the USDA National Plant Germplasm System. His work has been centered in Ames, Iowa, with the North Central Region Plant Introduction Station affiliated with Iowa State University, but David's impact has really been world-wide. He shares amaranth seed with researchers around the world, is a hub of information on the crop through regular communication with amaranth workers, and has organized many amaranth meetings to share information on the crop. He also started the Amaranth Institute listserv, which is open to anyone to participate in. In writing this book, I consulted with David and a few others to get the latest information on amaranth. Jonathan and Larry Walters of Nu-World Foods were very helpful on amaranth processing and food markets. Pete Noll and Katherine Lorenz, who both have done some amazing work with amaranth in Mexico provided information on the work of the non-profit they have led, Puente a la Salud Comunitaria. Matthew Blair is one of the few university researchers currently working with amaranth, and I appreciate that he is working hard at Tennessee State University to research amaranth and breed new amaranth varieties.

The current status of amaranth in the U.S. and elsewhere in the world is based on earlier efforts of many people, too many to include here. However, I feel compelled to mention Dr. Dan Putnam, who first connected me to amaranth when he was an alternative crops researcher at University of Minnesota in the 1980s. Another key person in my early years of work was Dr. David Baltensperger, who was then a researcher on alternative crops at University of Nebraska and is now a department chair at Texas A & M University. David released the important variety of amaranth called Plainsman in 1992 and we exchanged a great deal of information on amaranth in the early 90s, later collaborating again in the early 2000s. Dr. Noel Vietmeyer, now retired, has been an inspiration to many researchers on alternative crops over the years through his books. Bob Rodale and his team of researchers at the Rodale Research Center (now the Rodale Institute), did a huge amount in the 1980s to not only rekindle interest in amaranth in the U.S. and other countries, but also conducted the foundational research upon which much progress with amaranth was based.

Lastly, I want to thank some key family members for their role in this book. My youngest daughter, Haley, now in her mid-20s, is a trained editor and far better writer than me, who served as the editor on this book, improving its quality significantly. She also did the page design and layout for the entire book, which was a huge help. My wife, Amy, served as a valuable proofreader, as she has on many other writing projects for me. She patiently put up with me being hidden away in my home study for many weekends writing this book, not to mention many years of growing amaranth in our gardens and other places. Her support and love through over the 35 plus years we've been together have been wonderful. My oldest daughter, Chelsea, contributed some artwork on amaranth to the book and has been a continuous creative inspiration to me. My mother-in-law, Marilyn Claus, helped motivate me to write the book because of her fascination with amaranth. My parents, Richard and Joan Myers, central Illinois grain farmers, both played a major role as well, with my dad teaching me much about farming over the years (he passed away in 2014), and my mom teaching me about gardening, flowers, and supporting my interest in books and learning.

Once people learn a little about amaranth, they usually want to know more. One of the more interesting historical tidbits I came across is that amaranth seeds for germination testing and amaranth cookies were actually sent into space on the Space Shuttle Atlantis in 1985. This was reportedly done to recognize Mexican astronaut Rodolfo Neri Vela who flew on that mission. Amaranth has periodically been the subject of other news pieces in the major media. In recent years, National Geographic, Forbes, Grist, and NPR have all run stories on amaranth.

I'll end this preface by sharing that for the last several years, I have served as Regional Director of Extension Programs with the North Central Region Sustainable Agriculture Research and Education (NCR-SARE) program, and also am an adjunct faculty member in plant sciences at University of Missouri. While my current job does not involve any formal responsibilities on amaranth, it does keep me in contact with researchers and farmers working to diversify farming operations. I continue to be inspired by the farmers I meet, and in a way, this book is a testament to them for their continued efforts to improve the sustainability of their farming operations. Finally, thanks to you as the reader for taking the time to learn more about amaranth, an amazing crop and food!

INTRODUCTION TO AMARANTH:
THE AZTEC "FOOD OF IMMORTALITY"

The true origins of amaranth use lie shrouded in the murky past of people living throughout the Americas millennia ago. However, one chapter in that history stands out in vivid relief, beginning November 8, 1519, when Hernan Cortez and his small army of Spanish conquistadors marched into the largest city in the Americas, Tenochtitlan. At the time, Tenochtitlan was five times larger than London, and at least equal in population to the largest cities in the world of that era, such as Paris and Naples. With 200,000 or more people in a capital city built on an island in a large lake of central Mexico, in the high mountain "Valley of Mexico," the impressive city with it's huge temples, canals, avenues, and elaborate art was awe-inspiring to the Spaniards. This island metropolis, capital of the advanced Aztec empire, was reachable only by causeways and bridges, and was a center of great wealth.

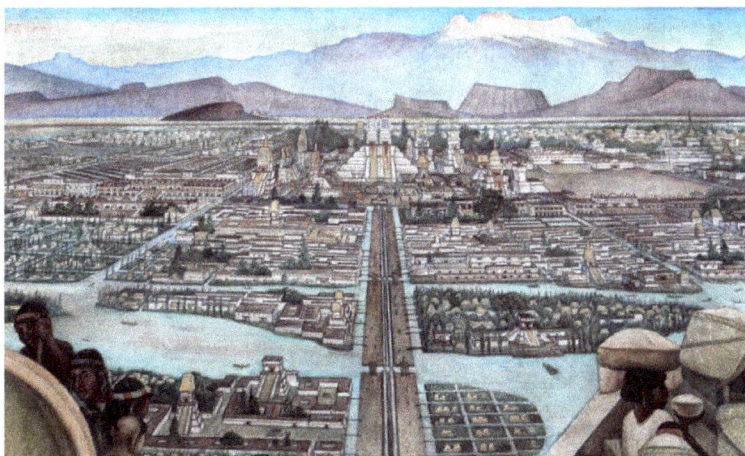

Artist rendering of the city of Tenochtitlan, capital of the Aztec empire where large amounts of amaranth were delivered in tribute to the Aztec Emperor. Tenochtitlan was one of the largest and most advanced cities in the world when the Spanish conquistadors arrived, and is the present day site of Mexico City, a metropolis of over 20 million people. The image above is from a 1952 fresco by Diego Rivera at the National Palace of Mexico.

Upon arriving on the island, some of the conquistadors felt they were dreaming, such was the magnificence of the city and culture they had come upon; in fact they called it the "The City of Dreams." A member of the Cortez expedition, Bernal Diaz, wrote:

> Gazing on such wonderful sights, we did not
> know what to say, or whether what appeared
> before us was real, for on one side, on the land,
> there were great cities, and in the lake ever so
> many more, and the lake itself was crowded with
> canoes, and in the Causeway were many bridges
> at intervals, and in front of us stood the great City
> of Mexico...

At the time of Spaniard arrival, there were two great crops supporting not only the Aztec capital city of 200,000, but also an empire estimated at 5 million people. One of those food crops was maize (corn), which had been adopted in much of North America hundreds of years earlier, and was soon to be spread by European ships throughout the world. The other crop was amaranth, called huauhtli by the Aztecs, which they also referred to as "the food of immortality." Surviving records indicate that the Aztec ruler, Montezuma, was given tribute of 20,000 tons of amaranth per year, which likely would have required 100,000 or more acres (40,000 hectares) of land to produce that much amaranth. Undoubtedly, a great deal of additional amaranth, possibly a million acres or more, was being grown just to help feed many others of the population of an estimated 5 million people who lived outside of the capital city.

At that moment in time, amaranth was perhaps the second most important food crop in the Americas after maize, and one of the most important in the world in supporting a major civilization. Unfortunately, within a few years of the conquistadors arrival, amaranth, the "everlasting flower," began to fade from human memory, only to reemerge in our time, nearly five centuries later.

In defeating and subjugating the Aztec people, Cortez and his conquistadors also sought to suppress their culture and eliminate many of their traditions. They leveled the temple complex at the center of Tenochtitlan, and built their new capital of Mexico City on top of the ruins. They took particular aim at the religion of the Aztecs, seeking to introduce Catholicism to the Aztecs.

While both maize and amaranth, as two of the major Aztec foods, were used in religious ceremonies, there are indications that amaranth played the far larger role in Aztec religion. The brilliantly colored flowers of amaranth likely contributed to that religious reverence. Records indicate that Aztec religious holidays also involved the creation of figurines made of amaranth seeds and honey. The seeds were likely popped first. Not unlike today's rice krispie bars, the sticky mass of popped amaranth seeds and honey could be made into various shapes and later eaten. A more disturbing image of those figurines is that some reportedly had blood mixed in with the amaranth and honey.

As the Spaniards moved to swiftly wipe away Aztec buildings, culture, and religion, in their ignorance they also swept away a vital food crop that could have helped many people over the subsequent centuries. According to at least one account, Cortez reportedly banned the production of amaranth by Aztec farmers on pain of death — talk about a tough government farm policy![1]

The question for us now is whether we have the foresight to recover the potential of amaranth for feeding millions of people around the world with a highly nutritious, adaptable crop. This fascinating food plant with brilliant crimson flowers and such a colorful past is the subject of this book. I hope you enjoy learning about amaranth as much as I have.

---

[1] *There is uncertainty over what the penalty for growing amaranth was since historical accounts differ. Regardless, actions of the conquistadors led to amaranth falling into disuse and being mostly forgotten until its resurrection in recent years.*

CHAPTER 1

THE PROMISE OF AMARANTH FOR MEETING NEEDS AROUND THE WORLD

On a sunny late summer day in 1987, I visited a farm in southern Minnesota. There, under a brilliant blue sky, was the most beautiful crop field I had ever seen. The large field had a million or more amaranth plants, and each head-high plant was topped by a crimson flowering seed head a foot or more in length. The combination of blue sky, puffy white clouds, and the sea of crimson flowers took my breath away. As I heard the farmer, Ed Hubbard, talk about his amaranth crop and its amazing history, I became completely fascinated. That colorful farm visit led to an irresistible urge to learn more about amaranth. Over 30 years later, and after a quarter-century growing amaranth, including many different research projects, my familiarity with amaranth has grown significantly. However, there is much, much more to be learned about this crop. In this book, I hope to share some of the things I've found so fascinating about amaranth, how you and others can eat it and even grow it, and why it has so much promise for the future.

Grain amaranth field in bloom.

What is amaranth?

There are a wide range of plants that are part of the amaranth botanical family, some of which are grown for seeds, others for leaves, several for flowers, and some are just wild plants that do their bit in the ecosystem. A few of the amaranths are troublesome weeds in some places, like pigweed and Palmer amaranth, but this book is not about them. Rather, most of the focus will be on grain amaranth grown for seed, though I'll make occasional reference to the vegetable amaranths from which leaves are eaten.

Human use of grain amaranths dates back at least 6000 years, and you can read all about the interesting history of amaranth in Chapter 6. Suffice it to say that in our current age, grain amaranth is being harvested for seed in many parts of the world, but mostly from modest numbers of farms in each region. The seed is mainly used for human food, in a wide range of food products. The plants are annuals that reach maturity in a single growing season. Grain amaranths are generally tall plants, typically 2 meters or more in height. The plants are vigorous and adaptable to a wide range of growing conditions, from lowlands to mountain valleys and dry areas to wetter humid regions. They are grown in both temperate and tropical parts of the world, both by hand and with machines. Amaranth is truly one of the most widely adapted crops that we have.

Why should you be interested in amaranth?

If you're like most people, you eat a variety of foods, try to get adequate nutrition, care at least a little that the environment is doing okay, and rely on farmers to produce your food, whether you think about them or not. Amaranth has a role to play in each of these areas, as I'll describe below. More specifically, in the rest of this chapter I'll address four general categories of people that can benefit from amaranth:

1. Consumers, especially those looking for healthier foods
2. Gardeners who like trying new colorful plants and/or growing their own food
3. Farmers, including those that want a diversified operation and low-input crops
4. Environmentalists, particularly people interested in the intersection of water, soil, and climate

Consumers and amaranth

We all eat, and we all want to be healthy. How many times have you seen the advice that you should eat a balanced diet with plenty of protein and moderate amounts of fats and carbohydrates, and you'll be fine? Oh, and you need some key vitamins and minerals, so you don't get bad things like scurvy that used to make sailors very sick when they went too long without Vitamin C from fruits. Did you know that people who rely too much on maize (corn) in their diet can develop malnutrition symptoms? Nursing mothers and children are particularly susceptible, and in some parts of the world, children eating mainly corn and not much else can end up much shorter, with other development issues as well. Those children are lacking not only adequate protein, but particularly two of the nine essential amino acids, lysine and tryptothan. They are also usually short in iron and key vitamins in their diet. One of the best foods to address these issues is amaranth, which is high in key vitamins and minerals, relatively good in iron, high in protein, and has an excellent balance of the nine essential amino acids. Of all the grains grown in the world, only amaranth and quinoa are close to milk in having the appropriate ratio of essential amino acids for human consumption.

To help malnourished children and other aspects of community health, a long-term effort has been made to reintroduce amaranth in Mexico, its native site of origin, by the organization Puente a la Salud Comunitaria. Their incredible work is the subject of Chapter 8, but for now, just be aware that adding a small amount

16

of amaranth to a corn-based diet appears to improve the health of malnourished children and nursing mothers. Their work needs to be replicated in more places, and I hope you'll enjoy reading about their uplifting story.

At this point you're thinking, okay, so amaranth helps people who are malnourished, but I don't have that problem. I'm glad to hear it! However, I bet you would like to eat foods that give you plenty of energy, protein, and other right "stuff" without causing you to gain a lot of extra weight. While I won't begin to promise that amaranth can solve the issue of being overweight, I can tell you that amaranth and quinoa have probably the best overall nutritional profile of any grains available to us today. You may have heard of quinoa as one of the latest superfoods that is growing by leaps and bounds in the food marketplace. You may even have had a quinoa burger or quinoa in your salad. What will probably surprise you is that you've probably eaten amaranth without even knowing it! Amaranth is gradually finding its way into more and more multi-grain products, often marketed as part of an "ancient grains" ingredient mix. After reading this book, I think you'll find yourself looking for more breads and other food products that include amaranth. Or you may find yourself buying some amaranth flour and making one of the tasty recipes at the end of this book.

Chapter 2 dives into the specifics of amaranth nutrition, but as a teaser for that chapter I'll tell you that amaranth has almost twice the protein content of corn, and your body makes more use of that protein because of the proper balance of amino acids. At this point, I need to make a quick disclaimer – I grew up on a corn and soybean farm, have done research on corn, regularly eat corn, and support the use of corn for many products – so my comparison of amaranth to corn isn't to downgrade corn, it's to show how much potential that amaranth has. As I pointed out in the introduction to the book, the real tragedy in the history of our foods is that we forgot about crops like amaranth and quinoa that came out of the same New World regions as corn and potatoes.

In Chapter 3, you'll learn about where you can find amaranth to eat, and what kinds of products you can find it in. The good news is that there are a variety of products that have amaranth in them, including breakfast cereals, breads, crackers, granola bars, and other snacks. Better yet, most grocery stores have amaranth flour and many have packaged amaranth grain, so you can buy and use nutritious amaranth in your own recipes.

Examples of products that include amaranth as an ingredient.

I will say that amaranth has a different taste from other grains, and like any food you're not used to, if you eat something that is mostly made from amaranth you will notice the taste difference. Some people like the taste right away and others may call it earthy or even less favorable terms! I myself prefer to have it blended with other grains or ingredients. For example, if you make chocolate chip or blueberry muffins with half wheat and half amaranth flour, you may detect a texture difference in the muffin but probably not a significant taste difference, because the strong flavor of the chocolate or blueberries masks the more subtle flavor of the amaranth.

Amaranth is gluten-free

For the majority of consumers, the overall nutrition of amaranth should be one of it's main selling points. For a subset of consumers, those who need or want gluten-free products, amaranth provides another grain alternative to wheat. Amaranth is completely gluten-free, and can be substituted for wheat in most recipes, although you can't make a raised loaf of bread from 100% amaranth flour. While there are other grains that are also gluten-free, for someone looking for diversity in their gluten-free food choices, amaranth is well worth considering, especially to add protein and general nutritional quality.

Gardeners and amaranth

Grain amaranths are a fun, easy, and low-cost plant to grow in your yard. Although you can start some plants out from seeds in pots and transplant a few into select sunny spots in the back of a flower border, I recommend growing at least a small area, such as a 4 by 4 foot raised bed, or maybe a larger patch if you have a good-sized vegetable garden. My primary vegetable garden area is about 30 by 40 feet. It's not uncommon for me to devote about half or more of that to sunflowers and amaranth. If planted at the same time, which for me is usually around June 1st, they will typically be flowering at the same time, or at least overlap (depending on the sunflower varieties used, some of which are early flowering than most grain amaranths). A patch of bright golden sunflowers next to some brilliant crimson or maroon amaranth flowers makes for quite a spectacle!

If you really are into growing your own food, or at least part of it, amaranth is an easier grain to harvest and thresh than something like wheat or oats (but not quite as easy as corn, I'll admit). You won't be able to grow a large amount of seed in a typical garden, but if you grow a 10 by 10 foot patch, you can reasonably expect to get a pound or more of seed. You can use the amaranth in your cooking in a few different ways (see the recipes at the end), including cooking the whole grain, popping the seeds, or grind them into flour. If you make your own flour with a table top grinder, be realistic about the amount of bread you can make. Perhaps 3 to 4 loaves of bread can be made from that 10 by 10 foot patch, but that's assuming that at least half the bread flour you are using is wheat.

A patch of grain amaranth can add vibrant color to the late summer garden.

Specifics on how to grow amaranth, both in a garden and in large farm fields, are provided in later chapters. If you are really short on space, just try one or a few plants in a pot. Since the plants can get tall, depending on the size of the pot, you may need to stake them if growing only one or a few at time, unless you have a sunny spot out of the wind.

You might also consider growing one of the vegetable amaranth varieties. Later chapters provide information on some of the considerations for growing and using vegetable amaranths. You can potentially get more food per unit of ground from the vegetable amaranths than the grain amaranths, and you don't have to go through the grain threshing process. The downside is that the vegetable amaranths are not as showy in terms of flowers and size as the grain amaranths. You can eat grain amaranth leaves, but pick the younger, more tender leaves. Also, it's best to cook the grain amaranth leaves like spinach before eating to avoid any potential issues from nitrates or oxalates that might accumulate in the leaves.

Several garden seed companies sell amaranth seed. I go into details on obtaining seed in Chapter 5 on amaranth varieties. Regardless of where you get seed from, I encourage you to try a few different amaranth varieties. Amaranth varieties come in a variety of flower colors, and some vary in leaf color and plant height as well.

If you are thinking you've grown amaranth in your garden before, most likely you grew an ornamental type of amaranth rather than true grain amaranth. Many people have grown a cousin of grain amaranth called "Love-lies-bleeding" and you may have grown small "globe amaranth," which is an even more distant cousin of grain amaranth, part of a different genus of plants but still part of the highly diverse Amaranthaceae family. Take a look at Chapter 4 on amaranth biology to learn more about some of the many different types of amaranth.

Farmers and amaranth

I've enjoyed helping several grain farmers who have tried growing amaranth, and generally they find it comparable to growing other summer grain crops and quite feasible to produce. I go into all the details about how to grow amaranth commercially in Chapters 9-12, but in this brief section want to address why farmers should consider growing amaranth.

The basic reasons a farmer should consider growing grain amaranth are that it is a low-input, low-cost crop to grow that adds biodiversity to a farming operation. It works well in rotation with other row crops such as corn, sorghum, small grains, and soybeans, and in southern areas can be double cropped after winter wheat. It can be grown with the same equipment as these other crops. Only two pounds of seed are needed per acre which can keep seed costs low. Fertility needs are modest, the crop competes well with weeds, and irrigation is seldom-needed unless growing in the most moisture-deficient areas. Amaranth is widely adapted, and just as importantly, is tolerant of dry weather, which is the type of trait needed in many farming regions.

However, it's no slam dunk to adopt, or everyone would be growing it, right?! The number one limitation from a farming standpoint is the lack of current markets. It gets expensive to ship grain hundreds of miles, and right now there are very few companies taking truckloads of amaranth as unprocessed grain in the U.S. (although there are many food companies using minor amounts of amaranth flour). An enterprising farmer might be able to direct retail a modest volume of amaranth seed, but like creating any new venture, building up a market can take time.

Even if the market problems are solved, there are some challenges in growing amaranth. There are no registered herbicides for amaranth. That won't bother an organic farmer, but for others, that's a limitation. Fortunately, there are ways to grow amaranth successfully without herbicides (see Chapter 11). Harvesting amaranth with a combine is not too difficult, but getting the seed reasonably clean and free from foreign material, a requirement for most buyers, is more challenging and requires some planning and possibly some trial and error with seed cleaning. Details on harvesting and seed storage are in Chapter 12.

Overall, for any grain farmer considering amaranth, I'd say the following. By all means, do a little experimentation with amaranth. Plant some in your garden, or maybe a strip along the edge of a field (just be careful what broadleaf herbicides may be sprayed near it!). Maybe the first year you plant a strip of amaranth with a planter, you shouldn't even worry about harvesting it, just learn how it grows and watch how it matures. If you want to take the next step, and grow a few acres for harvest, figure out your cleaning and storage plans in advance, and most importantly, identify your market before planting! I would not encourage anyone to jump in with a 40-acre field of amaranth before gaining some experience. That would likely not end well. But with a couple of years of experience, plenty of farmers have become successful at growing the crop. Just keep in mind that markets are currently quite limited, so building the markets is at least half the battle in using amaranth as a crop.

Amaranth on the left and soybeans on the right, looking comparable in mid-summer, but soon after this point the amaranth will quickly outgrow the soybeans and reach 6 feet or more in height.

Farmers and researchers viewing amaranth varieties at the Plant Introduction Station in Ames, IA.

Environmentalists and amaranth

Most farmers try to do a good job as stewards of the land, but modern agriculture has its share of environmental issues. The impact of fertilizers on water quality is one of the most frequently studied and discussed problems. Crops like amaranth that have modest fertility needs are helpful in that regard because less fertilizer is put on for the crop. My own research on nitrogen fertility needs with amaranth showed that 80 pounds of nitrogen per acre was plenty on central Missouri soils, about half what is put on corn. On the other hand, corn produces far more grain per acre than amaranth.

Amaranth is also unlikely to be sprayed with much in the way of agricultural chemicals, mainly because there are very few synthetic farm chemicals labeled for legal use with amaranth. About half the farmers I have encountered growing amaranth over the years were producing it organically, but the rest used synthetic nitrogen and got by with either organic insecticides or didn't spray anything at all. They might have used glyphosate as a "burn-down" herbicide before planting amaranth, which is allowed. So bottom line, very few chemicals, if any, get put on amaranth fields.

The biggest benefit of amaranth for the environment, however, is its fit as a drought-tolerant crop that has low water needs. Given our changing climate, and the fact that more areas are experiencing short and long-term droughts, this is a critically important point for the future. Even in dry areas that normally have irrigation, we can expect the capacity to irrigate to become more limited in many areas in the future as groundwater aquifers get strained and surface waters decline or have more demands on them. In the Western U.S., water rights and access to water are already huge issues, and are likely to get even more contentious in the future. We are going to have more need of crops that can grow with limited rainfall and hot conditions as our climate continues to change. Amaranth can help meet that need.

CHAPTER 2

AMARANTH NUTRITION AND HEALTH

The excellent nutritional qualities of amaranth have captured many people's attention over the years. While no food is perfect, amaranth has a number of great qualities in terms of its nutritional characteristics. Among the nutritional qualities that stand out about amaranth are its protein, fiber, iron, and Vitamin E content. Its excellent nutritional profile and other seed characteristics have positive implications for human health, as I'll discuss later in this chapter. I'll start with a review of amaranth's basic nutritional profile.

The nutritional trait for which amaranth is most often acclaimed is the protein quality of its grain. Amaranth grain is 14-16% protein on a dry weight basis, which is a higher protein level than most cereal grains, and almost twice the protein percentage of corn (maize). However, amaranth is actually lower in protein than most legumes (beans can run 20% or more protein). Total protein level is only part of the story, however, since the composition of the protein in terms of essential amino acids is very important. In particular, amaranth has a great balance of the nine essential amino acids[1] that all people need in their diet. If a person eats a particular food that is low in one or more amino acids, the way corn is low in lysine and tryptophan, it can significantly limit the value of the protein being consumed, unless the deficient amino acid(s) are made up for by other foods. In parts of the world where the diet is heavily based on corn, such as parts of Africa and parts of Mexico, children can end up being malnourished even though they are getting adequate calories, partly because corn they are eating is deficient in lysine and tryptophan.

---

1 *The nine essential amino acids for humans in their diet are histidine, isoleucine, leucine, lysine, methionine, phenylalanine, threonine, tryptophan, and valine. Essential amino acids are ones that humans cannot synthesize on their own from other food sources and thus need to have as part of the diet to maintain good health.*

Traditionally, a different food such as beans are eaten with corn to help offset the deficiencies of corn. Beans also have their own deficiencies, being particularly low in methionine, which corn has adequate amounts of.

I should add that deficiencies in amino acids are often only part of what causes malnutrition. Malnourished children in areas that have a corn or cassava-based diet also can need more dietary fats, and often need more Vitamin A, zinc, and iron. Amaranth is a good way to help provide these key nutrients, as amaranth has up to 3x the iron, higher zinc, and 30-40% more dietary fat than corn. Reports from field workers in Mexico and east Africa have indicated very promising results from including a modest amount of amaranth in a corn-based diet, but more research is needed to better understand the level of amaranth needed and the health benefits that can be obtained.

The picture with Vitamin A from amaranth is more unclear. The USDA nutrient database shows only a very low level of Vitamin A, but in tests we had through the University of Missouri Analytical Chemistry Lab, values were considerably higher. The USDA database does show good value of Vitamin A in amaranth leaves, with 3656 IUs of Vitamin A in a cup of cooked amaranth leaves, equivalent to about 73% of the recommended daily allowance for Vitamin A. More research on Vitamin A content and levels of Vitamin A precursors in grain amaranth would be welcome.

Going back to protein, what's unique about amaranth, and its distant cousin quinoa (both members of the same plant family), are that amaranth and quinoa are both so well-balanced in the nine essential amino acids. In fact, some nutritionists have compared them to milk in the quality of the protein. That means that amaranth grain is a great complement to other foods that are deficient in certain amino acids, or can be used as a primary source of a "complete" protein. More details on amaranth's amino acid profile and other nutritional characteristics can be found in a recent review article by Venskutonis and Kraujalis (2013).

In terms of overall protein, amaranth ranks ahead of most other grains that are ground into flour and used for baking. Protein level of grain amaranths, as with other grains, depends on the variety, growing region, and weather conditions that year. The USDA reported protein level for grain amaranth is 13.56%[2], which may be based on amaranth imported to the U.S., and is lower than many other reported values for amaranth protein; in my own testing of grain amaranth grown in Missouri, protein levels were 15.5-16.2%. By comparison, USDA protein figures from the National Nutritional Database for some other common grains are whole grain cornmeal at 8.1%, brown rice at 7.5%, soft red wheat at 10.3%, durum wheat at 13.7%, and hard red wheat at 15.4%. Oats are the most competitive with total protein of amaranth, with the standard value of oats being 16.8% protein.

CROP->	Brown long grain rice	Hard red winter wheat	Yellow corn	Sorghum	Whole grain amaranth*	Golden Glow** amaranth	Amaranth Line 210
Protein %	7.54	12.61	9.42	10.62	13.56	15.5	16.2
Fat %	3.20	1.54	4.74	3.46	7.02	6.8	6.4
Iron mg	1.29	3.19	3.36	3.36	7.61	8.80	11.8
Zinc mg	2.13	2.65	2.21	1.67	2.87	4.5	3.5
Calcium mg	9	29	7	13	159		
Vitamin B6 mg	0.477	0.30	0.622	0.443	0.591		

Table 1. A comparison of various varieties of amaranth to other grains for selected nutrients. The last two columns on the right show that variation is available within amaranth breeding lines, so selection for certain nutrients could lead to increased values if desired for certain uses.
* The "whole grain amaranth" column is from the USDA National Nutrient Database – exact type of amaranth represented is unknown. Notably the protein percent is lower than many other reported values for amaranth.
** The columns starting with "Golden Glow amaranth" and the 210 experimental amaranth line are data from the University of Missouri Chemical Services Lab.

2 *National Nutrient Database for Standard Reference Legacy Release April 2018, U.S. Department of Agriculture, Agriculture Research Service. Online database.*

However, oats are somewhat deficient in the essential amino acids lysine and threonine.

Another takeaway from the data we collected on several different amaranth genotypes is that there is plenty of genetic variation to work with in the amaranth germplasm for improved nutritional traits. Some experimental lines out of crosses in the small amaranth breeding effort I've run showed that key traits such as iron, zinc, squalene, and Vitamin A can vary quite a bit. Thus, if a breeder really wanted to maximize any of these constituents, it appears they could make good headway through further breeding with grain amaranth.

The USDA Nutrient Database has information on 16 different species of grains, including 4 kinds of wheat. Among those, amaranth ranked highest of all the grains for Vitamin C, Vitamin B6, lipids (dietary fats), magnesium, and phosphorous. It essentially tied with teff for being highest in iron, an important trait for dealing with malnutrition (amaranth had 3.42 mg of iron per FDA unit, while teff had 3.43, whereas the next highest grain was quinoa at 2.06 mg). Thus, amaranth led among grains for 5 categories of nutrients and was almost tied for a sixth. Quinoa, by contrast led just two categories, while teff and buckwheat led three categories each. Amaranth was also rated good in protein, fiber, copper, and selenium. In short, amaranth is an exceptional food from a nutritional standpoint.

Directly comparing amaranth and quinoa

Many people interested in healthy grains have tried quinoa, and a fair number are using quinoa regularly in their diet. From my perspective, anyone who is motivated to try quinoa should also give amaranth a try in their diet. These two ancient grains are more alike than they are different, and in several regards are very similar from a nutritional standpoint. Among the true cereal grains and pseudocereals, amaranth and quinoa have the most balanced amino acid profile for human needs, as was identified earlier. They are also very high in protein to begin with compared to other grains, though lower than most legumes. Table 3 below shows quinoa having slightly higher protein, but most other published sources on amaranth grain have protein percent-

Table 2

Nutrient	% DV
Protein	52%
Fat	21%
Carbohydrate	42%
Dietary fiber	52%
Vitamins	
Vitamin A	0%
Vitamin C	14%
Vitamin D	-
Vitamin E	11%
Vitamin K	0%
Thiamin	15%
Riboflavin	22%
Niacin	9%
Vitamin B6	57%
Folate	40%
Vitamin B12	0%
Pantothenic acid	28%
Minerals	
Calcium	31%
Iron	82%
Magnesium	120%
Phosphorous	108%
Potassium	28%
Sodium	0%
Zinc	37%
Copper	51%
Manganese	322%
Selenium	52%

Table 3

Nutrient	Amaranth	Quinoa
Protein (g)	13.6	14.1
Fat (g)	7.0	6.1
Carbohydrate (g)	65.7	64.2
Dietary fiber (g)	6.7	7.0
Vitamins		
Vitamin A (IU)	2	14
Vitamin C (mg)	4.2	-
Vitamin D	-	-
Vitamin E (mg)	1.2	2.4
Vitamin K (mcg)	0.0	0.0
Thiamin (mg)	0.1	0.4
Riboflavin (mg)	0.2	0.3
Niacin (mg)	0.9	1.5
Vitamin B6 (mg)	0.6	0.5
Folate (mcg)	82	184
Vitamin B12 (mcg)	0.0	0.0
Pantothenic acid (mg)	1.5	0.8
Minerals		
Calcium (mg)	159	47
Iron (mg)	7.6	4.6
Magnesium (mg)	248	197
Phosphorous (mg)	557	457
Potassium (mg)	508	563
Sodium (mg)	4.0	5.0
Zinc (mg)	2.9	3.1
Copper (mg)	0.5	0.6
Manganese (mg)	3.3	2.0
Selenium (mg)	18.7	8.5

Table 2. Amaranth contribution to nutrition as a percent of recommended daily values for adults based on a 2000 calorie diet. Portion of amaranth is one cup of uncooked grain (193 grams), which would provide 368 calories.
Source of data is the USDA Nutrition Database, version SR-21.

Table 3. Comparison of uncooked amaranth grain versus uncooked quinoa grain (100 mg of each).
Source of data is the USDA Nutrition Database, version SR-21.

age in the 14-16% range, which would make it equivalent to quinoa in protein or slightly higher. Based on the USDA Nutrition Database, amaranth is about 65% higher in iron than quinoa, is 20% higher in Vitamin B6, and has about 340% more calcium. They have almost identical levels of dietary fiber, while amaranth is slightly higher in dietary fat (both would be considered low fat products). Amaranth is higher in magnesium, phosphorous, manganese, and selenium, while quinoa is higher in Vitamin E, thiamin, riboflavin, niacin, folate, and potassium. Bottom line, they are both extremely nutritious food sources.

Besides nutrition, one other comparison worth making between amaranth and quinoa is their regions of adaption. Quinoa is a crop that fares best in high mountain elevations, such as where it originated in the South America Andes Mountains, or other areas that have cooler summers. Amaranth is much more widely adapted in terms of growing regions, doing well at high and low elevations and being tolerant of hot conditions. From my trials in Missouri, amaranth performs much better than quinoa, but it may be that through future plant breeding efforts, quinoa varieties can be developed that are better suited to hotter low elevation conditions.

The grains do differ a bit in their acceptability to the human palate and functionality in cooking. Quinoa contains saponins that require pre-treatment to remove. This can be done at home by rinsing and then soaking the seeds for 12 to 24 hours, or can be done commercially by washing and milling. Amaranths don't have any problem with saponins, but do have a stronger taste than quinoa. Some people would say quinoa has a milder taste, and amaranth more grassy or earthy. The earthy taste of amaranth can be reduced by toasting the flour, giving it a more nutty taste, and is often masked in multi-ingredient foods by stronger tastes from ingredients such as chocolate, cinnamon, cheese flavoring, or fruits in baked or processed foods. Quinoa seed, while small, is about twice the size of amaranth seed, allowing it to be a little easier to use as a rice substitute, while amaranth can be used in polenta recipes. Both grains can be popped or puffed which can improve their flavor and add crunchiness to some recipes. They are both versatile and can be used in a wide variety of recipes – try some of each!

Future research needs on amaranth nutrition and health

I've already made mention of the interesting results from adding amaranth to the diet of malnourished children in Africa and Mexico. Similar positive results have been seen with adding amaranth to the diet of lactating mothers who were suffering from malnutrition. However, the research in these situations has been limited and much more work is needed before simply declaring that amaranth is the solution to malnutrition.

Likewise, there have been reports of amaranth helping with other medical issues. Some of these are perhaps based on people switching to a gluten free diet with amaranth as a gluten free food source. Others may be based on other nutritional components. The idea of nutraceuticals in our foods has been raised by some, such as the higher level of antioxidants found in blueberries and other foods being beneficial beyond normal protein, fat, carbohydrate, and vitamin considerations. Essentially, the theory of nutraceuticals is that some foods may act as alternatives to certain pharmaceuticals. The use of plants to cure a variety of ills is certainly not new, but dates back throughout human history. The main take away I want to leave the reader with is that there are a number of promising implications that have been seen with amaranth for human health, but much more research is needed.

CHAPTER 3
CURRENT USES OF AMARANTH FOR FOOD AND OTHER PRODUCTS

As elaborated on in the next chapter on amaranth history, the seeds or grain of amaranth have been used as a human food for thousands of years. The use of amaranth leaves as a green vegetable also likely dates back thousands of years. While both the grain and vegetable uses of amaranth continue to this day, amaranth has also gained use as an ornamental plant, increasingly planted in gardens for its colorful flowers and sometimes as a cut flower. The brilliant colors of the flowers, and in some varieties, the colored leaves, provide a potential source of plant-based dyes as well. These various uses are discussed in more depth in this chapter. Most of the information on amaranth use in commercial products in this chapter is focused on the U.S., since I have more direct access to those productions and information. In other countries, there could be other types of products besides what is mentioned below.

Amaranth grain

In general, amaranth grain is used in many of the same ways as cereal crops such as wheat and oats. Most often, the grain is ground into a flour which has excellent functional characteristics for baking. Lacking gluten, a bread made with 100% amaranth will not make a raised loaf, but various flatbreads can be made. Alternatively, the amaranth flour can be mixed with wheat flour at up to 50% and still produce a raised loaf of bread, albeit with less loft and more density than a 100% wheat loaf.

One functional characteristic of amaranth that distinguishes it from many other cereals is the fact it can be popped and used as a whole seed product in that way. It can also easily be puffed, similar to puffed rice, just with a much smaller seed size. Being able to pop or puff amaranth seeds increases the range of possible food uses for amaranth besides just using it as a ground flour. Also, the seeds can be cooked into a porridge with water and typically some milk, perhaps with a bit of sweetener such as brown sugar.

The gluten free nature of amaranth was discussed at some length in the previous chapter on nutrition, but it's worth repeating here that a driving force in the use of amaranth grain in food products has been that it is a gluten-free high-protein food source. As more and more people are looking for gluten-free products, this is creating an opportunity for more products using grain amaranth. In fact, I would suggest that the use of amaranth for the gluten-free market has barely been tapped, so for any entrepreneurs reading this book – here's your opportunity!

Sandwich breads

In the U.S., amaranth flour is used for a wide variety of products. It's often part of multigrain sandwich breads, although it may be the 10th or 11th grain in the mix by percentage due to relatively high cost and limited availability. Companies such as Pepperidge Farm have long made a multi-grain sandwich bread that includes amaranth, and now a number of smaller bread makers such as Dave's Organic Bread are using amaranth in some of their products as well.

If you like to make your own sandwich bread, you'll find a recipe suggestion at the end of the book as part of the recipe section. Of course, there are many more recipes on the internet for bread incorporating amaranth. Many of these recipes will use amaranth as about a fourth of the overall flour mixture, with the rest coming from wheat flour. At that percentage, the bread will raise about as well as normal, but have a slightly different texture. In general, you can go up to about half of the flour mix with amaranth, the rest being wheat; just expect that the loaf will not raise as much with that percentage of amaranth flour, and at that level of composition, the amaranth will have more of a taste impact. If you find you like the nutritional benefits of amaranth but aren't totally wild about the flavor, you can easily mask the flavor of the amaranth by including other ingredients in the bread (raisins, dried fruit, etc.) or just cut back on the percent of amaranth in the bread mix. Also, toasting amaranth flour before baking with it can reduce the "earthy" flavor.

Amaranth is sometimes used in multi-grain breads, such as the Pepperidge Farm 15 Grain Bread on the left. Many grocery stores also carry whole grain amaranth flour for home baking.

Breakfast cereals

Amaranth has also been available in selected breakfast cereals for a number of years. Although not as commonly found as sandwich breads that have amaranth, you can often find at least one or two breakfast cereal choices that include amaranth in the "health food" section of the grocery store. Just be aware that even some of the cereals labeled as "amaranth cereal" usually have some other grain, such as oats or wheat, as the primary ingredient. Again, this is due to the higher cost of amaranth flour compared to more commonly available grains. The most common amaranth breakfast cereals have been "amaranth flakes." Brand names of amaranth flake breakfast cereal makers include Arrowhead Mills, Health Valley, and Nature's Path. Additional companies like Van's offer other types of breakfast cereals that include amaranth.

Front and side of box of Van's "Cinnamon Heaven" multi-grain cereal including amaranth.

Granola bars

Over the last decade or two there has been a veritable explosion in offerings of all types of granola bars or other food bars, many custom-marketed to particular audiences, such as those wanting a trail bar, high-protein bar, energy bar, low-fat bar, or breakfast bars. Although amaranth has been used a little in multi-grain granola bars, this is an area ripe for more use of amaranth. Over the years, I've worked quite a bit with agricultural economist

Alan Weber, who also farms part-time in Missouri. In a joint project we did with USDA funding in the early 2000s, Alan assessed the economic opportunities for grain amaranth in various food products and concluded that food bars were the easiest entry point for small companies wishing to incorporate amaranth and find new market niches. This is particularly because of the very high nutritional qualities of amaranth, but also because it's ability to be puffed or popped as well as used as a flour gives a variety of options for putting it into a food bar. An example of a company that is making use of amaranth is Pure Organic, which has a line of "Ancient Grains" food bars.

There are many recipes available to make your own food bar using amaranth as part of the ingredients. Some of the options are no-bake and others require baking. The nice thing is that adding amaranth to the ingredient mix is a great way to boost the nutritional quality of the bar. By using puffed or popped amaranth you can also add some interesting texture to the bar.

Crackers

Over the years, a variety of cracker products have been made that included some amaranth. I don't believe I've ever seen any that were 100% amaranth, probably because of the cost of amaranth, but technically it would be possible to make a 100% amaranth cracker. Instead, amaranth shows up in a number of cracker products as part of multi-grain blends, many of them marked as "ancient grains" products. For example, at the time of this writing, Nabisco was offering a version of their popular Wheat Thins cracker called "Good Thins," with a subheading of "Ancient Grains." Clearly some food companies have latched onto the marketing appeal of these ancient grains.

As with other food products mentioned above, amaranth is unfortunately only a minor ingredient of this particular cracker: in the order of other grains used in that "Good Thins: Ancient

Grains" cracker, from those used the most to the least, are wheat, oats, buckwheat, millet, quinoa, amaranth (see photo below). In looking at other crackers on the market that contain amaranth, and there are quite a few, I did come across an interesting dinosaur-shaped Target store brand cracker with amaranth called "Puffed Ancient Grain Dino Snack." Even bigger than the title on the bag is the phrase "Super foods." I found curious that the "ancient grains" were not listed on the front of the product, but the ingredients "tomato, basil, and cheddar" were promoted on the front. The world of food marketing is an interesting one!

Front and back side of "Good Thins Ancient Grains" crackers made partially from amaranth.

Other baked foods or snacks

While I focused on sandwich breads, cereals, crackers, and food bars above, there's no doubt that amaranth can be used in any number of other types of food products. Basically, anywhere wheat, oats, rice, or corn are used, amaranth can be substituted, at least for part of the recipe. I haven't too often come across amaranth in bread products outside of sandwich breads, but there's no reason amaranth can't be used in rolls, bagels, muffins, pita bread, and other flat breads or specialty bread products. Likewise, amaranth can be used in puffed or extruded food products like cheese puffs. Many years ago I was at an amaranth conference at University of Minnesota, and a food scientist who had worked with amaranths let us try some cheese puff type products made from 100% amaranth. He said the amaranth worked very well in the extruder that made the cheese puff products. He gave us both plain ones and ones that had been coated in the typical cheese powder. I did not particularly care for the plain ones, but the cheese coated ones tasted much like regular cheese puffs. As he said, add enough cheese flavoring and almost anything will taste good!

Amaranth as part of a vegetarian meat substitute

One of the new uses of amaranth has been to include it as an ingredient in products made as meat substitutes. This is not widely done yet, although the high protein content of amaranth and diverse ways it can be used make it promising for this food role. An example of a company using amaranth is Gardein out of Vancouver, Canada. One of their products with amaranth I've eaten is "Seven Grain Crispy Tenders," which is like a breaded chicken strip product. In the future, I expect we'll see more use of high protein grains like amaranth and quinoa in meat substitute products.

Where to get amaranth seeds, flour, and mixed grain food products

In addition to looking for food products that include amaranth, I encourage you to try incorporating it into some of your own cooking. Amaranth flour is available in most grocery stores, sometimes in their health food aisle rather than next to regular wheat flour. Often the same sections of those grocery stores will also carry whole seed amaranth and at least a few specialty multi-grain products with amaranth. Of course, stores that specialize in health food will typically carry a variety of specialty grain food products, including amaranth. You can also order amaranth flour from online sources. Bob's Red Mill is a company that has sold amaranth flour and bagged amaranth seeds (grains) for many years, both in grocery stores and online.

Pet foods with amaranth

Cost is always an understandable consideration for food manufacturers. I was somewhat surprised to find out that premium pet food manufactures, while still cost-conscious, are perhaps more willing to pay a high price for their ingredients than human food manufacturers. On the other hand, when you think about how people are with their pets, including me, cost is not always a huge factor. So amaranth has occasionally popped up in premium pet foods, although I think the short supply of amaranth is limiting the number that are currently using it. Blue Buffalo, which carries a wide range of dog food, currently offers an amaranth-containing dog food under the name "Blue Buffalo Earth's Essentials Mountaintop Medley Lamb & Barley Ancient Grains Recipe Dry Dog Food." Belcando is a German-made dog food that includes amaranth and other premium ingredients. I suspect there are likely other pet foods on the market that also have amaranth as a minor constituent in the ingredients.

Vegetable amaranths

To my knowledge, vegetable amaranths have not entered the mainstream processed food industry in the U.S. However, they are becoming more common at farmers' markets, and sometimes are sold as a fresh leafy green in food stores, especially those that carry some local farm products. Typically, vegetable amaranths are cooked liked spinach, in part because the cooking removes any excess nitrates or oxalates that might have accumulated in the leaves. Some people use vegetable amaranth leaves along with other mixed vegetables in stir fry.

Vegetable amaranth still does not have the popularity or even familiarity to people in the U.S. that it does in many other parts of the world, including the Caribbean, Southeast Asia, and parts of Africa. Where it is most popular in the U.S. is where there are immigrants from the afore-mentioned regions of the world, typically in some of the larger U.S. cities that have a concentrations of immigrants who are creating enough demand for local farmers to prioritize growing some vegetable amaranths.

Could vegetable amaranth be the next kale in terms of interest and popularity? It certainly has good nutrition, but there would need to be simultaneous growth of production and demand to get it into more market outlets. Given the growing interest in "Asian" vegetables and other novel foods in Western countries, I expect the use of vegetable amaranth will expand.

Amaranth for floral use and dyes

Although some of the ornamental garden types of amaranth, such as Love-lies-bleeding (Amaranthus caudatus) are occasionally used for fresh flower arrangements, it's my impression that there is very little use of the showy grain amaranth flowers in the commercial florist industry; at least that appears to be the case in the U.S. I attribute this to a lack of awareness of amaranth and a lack of growers producing it for that market. While grain amaranth inflorescences are not necessarily the ideal flower in that they can be overly large and start to droop after several days, they do have two unique things going for them. First, the fact that they can be picked as particularly large flowers can provide for a showy bouquet. I've often gathered grain amaranth inflorescences that were 16-18 inches long and 8-10 inches thick. Just a few of those in a vase makes quite an impression.

Even more significantly, amaranth flowers can keep their color for an extended period. If cut fresh from the field or garden, and put in water, they will look good for several days but then start drooping like most other cut flowers. However, if cut at the right time (before seed forms) and handled carefully, they will keep the majority of their color and structure as a flower, sometimes for many months. Most other fresh flowers just turn brown after a week or so and fall apart. The photo below of a pair of grain amaranth inflorescences I had given my mother-in-law, with the first photo taken shortly after they were cut, the second photo from eight months later. The color is somewhat less brilliant than when they were first cut, but still nice.

The bright color of both amaranth flowers and the red pigment in the leaves of some varieties comes from anthocyanins. These anthocyanins have real potential value as non-toxic, plant-based dyes. To my knowledge, amaranth has not been used widely as a source of dye in modern times, although there is some evidence that the Aztecs used it as a dye. More research on the

Grain amaranth flowers fresh picked with some zinnias on the left. On the right are the same amaranth flowers 8 months later, still showing some decent color and holding together well, though a bit droopier. This illustrates why amaranth is called the "everlasting flower."

use of amaranths as a dye source certainly seems merited. I was intrigued to come across a research article (Godibo et al., 2015) where scientists had tested five different plant-based dyes for improving the efficiency of solar cells. Among the dyes they tested, *Amaranthus caudatus* provided the best efficiency for solar cells. This is important because current coloring of solar cells is typically done with products that contain heavy metals, which can cause environmental contamination when discarded. They concluded from their research that the amaranth dye would be an environmentally-friendly and cost-effective alternative to the heavy metal color tinting being done in solar cells.

CHAPTER 4

BIOLOGY AND TYPES OF AMARANTH

One of the things I have found most interesting about amaranth over the years is the genetic diversity, not just within the grain amaranths, but among the amaranth botanical family as a whole. While this chapter will focus mainly on the grain types of amaranth, I'll briefly address some of the vegetable and ornamental types of amaranth as well. First, I'll start off with some general information on the biology and growth characteristics of the grain amaranths, followed by an overview of the botanical species (types) of amaranth. In the chapter following this one I'll follow up on this discussion about the various types of amaranth with more detailed information on amaranth varieties.

Amaranth biology and growth characteristics

The grain amaranths, and indeed all of the cultivated types of amaranth, are warm season annual plants, which means they grow best in the heat of summer and need only one growing season to reach maturity and produce seeds before dying. They are broadleaf plants, which is exactly as it sounds, meaning they have leaves that are wide as opposed to narrow-leafed grasses. In terms of seed emergence, they are considered dicots, which indicates that there are two cotyledons (seed leaves), and those cotyledons have epigeal emergence, meaning the cotyledons come above ground.

Grain amaranth seeds are tiny, round, and light-colored, varying from tan to off-white or cream-colored. They are typically about 1 mm (0.04 inch) in diameter and weigh about 1 mg each (smaller than clover or mustard seeds). The seeds have an endosperm that wraps around the seed in an equatorial or belted fashion. Seeds of grain amaranth cultivars do not have dormancy, meaning that shortly after harvest they can be planted and will grow. Once upon a time I did some testing with several varieties of grain amaranth at various temperatures in a controlled seed germinator machine, and found that those cultivars germinated best starting around 68 degrees F (20 degrees C) or above. In Missouri that means they won't normally grow if planted in cool soils in April, that they might come up if planted in early May and you catch a warm spell, but it's best to plant later in May or even early June (see chapter on planting for many more details on how to grow amaranth). Besides just getting the seed germinated, the growing seedlings do better under warm temperatures. If it turns cool and wet after the seeds start to grow, "damping off" fungal diseases may attack and kill the seedlings.

One of the more unique characteristics of amaranth is that they are C4 plants, which means they use a very efficient biochemical pathway when making photoassimilates such as carbohydrates from sunlight. The C4 pathway is more common to tropical grasses such as corn (maize), millets, and sugarcane. Even wheat and rice, productive as they are, have only the C3 pathway, which is also true of soybeans, canola, and many other common crops. In fact, less than 5% of land plants have the efficient C4 photosynthetic pathway.

Growth characteristics

Grain amaranth cultivars are fast growing, with the exception of the first couple of weeks after emergence, while they are getting their roots established. It may seem when the plants first emerge they aren't doing much, but after a couple of weeks they will take off and start to grow rapidly. Compared to something like soybeans or garden beans, amaranth will grow more slowly at first, but by the time the beans are about 18 inches (45 cm) tall, the amaranth will be catching up and surpassing them. Grain amaranth height depends on both variety and soil conditions. Most varieties, when grown on a fertile, productive soil, will reach 6 1/2 feet or more in height (2 meters or more). On occasion, I've grown the same variety in multiple sites, and had them vary from 5 feet to as much as 7 feet or more in height (1.5-2.1 meters). I've seen some of those same varieties, such as Plainsman, in western Nebraska, where they grew only about 3 feet (1 meter) tall under much lower rainfall conditions.

Another thing I've noticed many times about amaranth is the interesting way it responds to overplanting and crowded plant conditions. As described in more detail in the chapter on amaranth planting, when many amaranth seeds are close together, during emergence from the soil a few of the plants will grow faster than the others in height, and soon leave the other plants in the dust. If there are 100 seeds planted in a foot of row, only one or two may reach full size, while most other seedlings will stay small or disappear. This is again a unique trait of amaranth. If you plant 100 corn seeds in a foot of row, they will all be overcrowded and stay much smaller than if spaced out. I did some testing years ago to determine if some seeds were genetically programmed to grow faster, and found out that it seemed to be much more a case of which plant had a little bit of a head start, maybe from being planted at a shallower depth, rather than any significant genetic difference in growth rate potential. All plants species have at least some phenotypic plasticity, meaning they alter growth in response to the environment, but amaranth seems to have it to a

Grain amaranth seeds and seedlings.

much higher degree than other annual crop plants. The practical implication is that it's easy to plant extra amaranth seeds and not worry about having to thin them out, unlike most garden plants. The amaranth will sort itself out and you end up with about the same number of mature plants whether you plant ¼ pound of seed per acre or 4 pounds of seed per acre (0.28 or 4.5 kg/ha).

The typical grain amaranth varieties have a single stalk and are unbranched with a single seed head (inflorescence). If you plant an amaranth variety that is normally unbranched and come across a branched plant with multiple seed heads, that's a weed—pull it out! Fortunately, such hybrids are normally either seedless or if they have seed, the seed will not germinate due to genetic incompatibilities of the parent plants (cultivated amaranth and weedy amaranth).

Grain amaranth varieties produce a lot of leaves, and if planted in rows about 30 inches wide (0.76 m), the leaves will fill that gap and totally shade the ground by the time flowering begins, such

Amaranth roots from plant in sandy loam soil on left. On the right, center plant is a weedy hybrid (infertile) with multiple branches and inflorescences instead of the normal single stalk and single inflorescence of grain amaranth varieties.

as late July or early August, assuming adequate soil moisture and fertility.

The root system of amaranth is highly branched and will normally include a larger tap root that goes more-or-less straight down. I'd love to see a good study on how the rooting depth of amaranth compares to other crops, but based solely on digging up amaranth and other crops over the years, I'd guess that amaranth is roughly equivalent to soybeans in its rooting depth.

One year I had an interesting research study where I planted amaranth side by side with several other crops in a University of Missouri research field that had been altered by an earlier researcher to have different depths of topsoil down to an impermeable plant layer. The soil depths ranged from about a foot down to three feet (0.9 m). We happened to have a dry summer, so as the summer progressed, the plants got noticeably short on water, first on the shallower top soil depths, then eventually even on the three foot depths. Of about 8 crops grown, amaranth was the first to have leaves lose turgor pressure and wilt under moisture stress, which surprised me, because amaranth is considered relatively drought tolerant. After even the smallest rain, however, it would perk right back up and the leaves would look like nothing had happened with no tissue damage. Soybean leaves, on the other hand, were more likely to be permanently damaged and never recover after they have wilted.

My conclusion from that study was that under severe moisture stress, the amaranth plants' response mechanism is to have their leaves droop or wilt so that they stop transpiring water. By comparison, corn will roll its leaves under moisture stress. Somehow the viability of those amaranth leaves is maintained and they can quickly recover once some moisture is restored. Having said all this, it's important to note that I have never seen amaranth leaves under normal field conditions wilt quite so dramatically, so I feel that study was an extreme case created by the severe soil moisture limitations in that experimental field. More research on the drought tolerance mechanisms of amaranth and its rooting system is worth exploring.

Flowering

In my area, amaranth planted around June 1 starts to produce a small inflorescence (flowering head) at the top of the plant towards the end of July. That inflorescence will quickly grow in size, and typically reaches full size by mid to late August. Each inflorescence is composed of thousands of tiny individual flowers, with a mix of both male and female flowers. The female flowers will develop into tiny seeds if pollinated properly. Amaranth plants are primarily self-pollinated, meaning that flowers are normally fertilized by pollen coming from the same plant.

Unlike many other seed producing plants, amaranth inflorescences stay colorful while seed are being formed. Most other plants that produce seeds have a shorter period of flowering and then the flower petals drop off and the seed develops. With amaranth, most of the colorful flower petals and components stay in place during seed development.

Photoperiod

The factors affecting the timing of amaranth flowering are not well studied. Generally, for most plant species, either day length (really, night length is the key) and/or the amount of heat accrued during the growing season will affect the timing of flowering. Although I can't say for absolutely certain what drives amaranth flowering, after observing flowering on the *A. hypochondriacus* grain amaranths for over 25 years, here's my theory. That species of amaranth, when planted early in summer, appears to flower after it accumulates enough heat units; there may still be a a requirement for a lengthening night period, but heat over time is the key trigger.

48

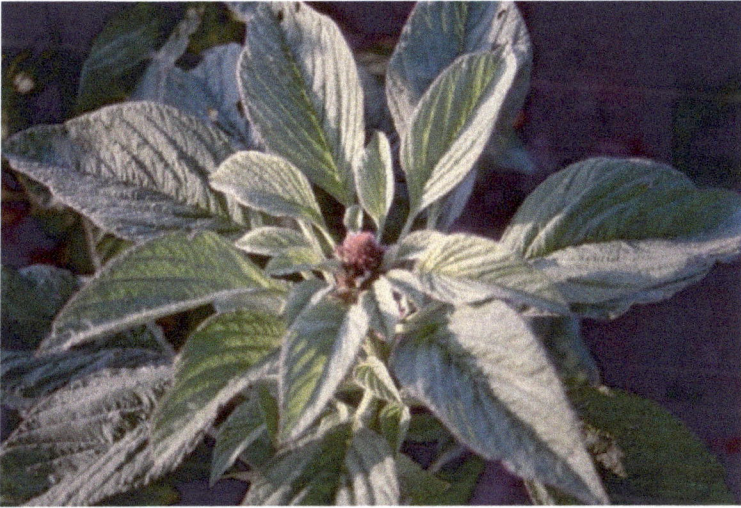

An amaranth inflorescence just emerging. Within a few weeks the inflorescences will often be a foot or more in length.

However, if the *A. hypochondriacus* species of amaranth is planted later in the summer, then it appears night length becomes overriding in importance for triggering flowering. I say this because I've had planting date studies and other situations where I had the same varieties of amaranth planted on multiple dates growing side by side. The earlier plantings flowered earlier than the late plantings, but it was clear the plants needed to get a certain amount of vegetative growth before starting to flower (accumulating those heat units). On the other hand, when I've planted amaranth in the latter part of July, it will start flowering very quickly, such as a foot or two tall (0.3-0.6 m). So it still accumulates some heat units before flowering (in other words, it doesn't flower a few days after emergence), but it happens much faster than when planted early in the season. For the home gardener or farmer, the takeaway is to plant by early or mid-June in order to get adequate vegetative growth on the plants before they start to flower and produce seed.

Seed development and seed color

The grain amaranths grown in the U.S. and temperate areas are normally *A. hypochondriacus,* and those have an indeterminate flower development pattern, meaning that not all flowers mature at exactly the same time. This is true of the seeds as well, that depending on when an individual flower was pollinated, that flower will develop into a seed earlier or later than others. Some of the *A. cruentus* types may be more determinate in their flowering pattern. In the cultivated amaranths, as was noted earlier, all the seeds are light colored, compared to the black seed of wild amaranths. I've heard some food buyers say they like the lighter color of quinoa compared to amaranth. I expect it would be possible to achieve lighter colored amaranth seed through breeding, whiter than the typical cream or tan color, but to most people the seed and processed flour color is quite acceptable.

Later in this book, in the chapter on harvesting, I'll describe in more depth the visual cues I've learned to use to tell when amaranth seeds are mature, but to summarize briefly here, it's a change from a translucent or glossy seed appearance to an opaque or non-glossy appearance. This visible change occurs because the starches in the seed are converting from a more liquid to solid form, not unlike corn seeds that go from the "milk stage" to the "dough stage." The amaranth seeds do not gain noticeably in size during this period, but they are becoming physiologically mature and reaching the point where they can be germinated to grow new plants.

Maturity and senescence

As grain amaranth plants reach maturity, assuming they have a long enough growing season before frost, the leaves will gradually fall off. Late in the fall, sometimes after or before frost (depending on growing region), the plants will completely senesce (die), and the stems, any remaining leaves, and the inflorescence (seed head) will turn completely tan or brown. Individual seeds will be mature well before this stage, some as much as a month before the seed head turns brown. Because the mature seeds

50

lose their physical connection to the rest of the seed head, they become at risk of falling to the ground (shattering). This is a normal evolutionary response in wild plants, that want to release their seeds to perpetuate the species. However, for us humans that want to be able to easily gather the seed, we'd rather the seeds stayed on the plant rather than falling to the ground, particularly tiny amaranth seeds! Fortunately, amaranth grain heads are sufficiently dense with flowers and plant material that most of the mature seeds are trapped in that mass of plant material up until the time the plant completely senesces (from frost or normal plant aging). At that point, with all the plant cells losing their turgor (water pressure), all bets are off, as the remaining plant tissues quickly dry down, shrivel, and seed starts quickly falling to the ground. So for both the home gardener and the farmer, timely harvest is important (see more on this in the chapter on harvesting).

Amaranth botanical types: relevant genera and species

Within the *Amaranthus* genus there are close to 70 different species of amaranths. In case you are fuzzy on your scientific classification system of taxonomy, keep in mind that the smallest taxonomic unit is a species, that multiple species make up each genus (plural is genera), and multiple genera make up a biological family. And yes, there is a broader amaranth family called Amaranthaceae, which contains something like 175 genera and 2500 total species! The broader Amaranthaceae family includes beets, sugar beets, quinoa, chard, spinach, and a number of ornamental plants, such as cockscomb (*Celosia* spp.) and globe amaranth (*Gophrena* spp.). My focus here will be on members of the *Amaranthus* genus, rather than the entire Amaranthaceae family. (In case you're wondering, species and genus names are supposed to be italicized, family names are not.)
If your head is spinning from how all these different plant names relate, it might help to picture that a house cat is a species (with the genus-species binomial for a house cat being *Felis catus*),

that all smaller cat species from Africa and southern Eurasia, both wild and domestic, are part of a genus (*Felis*), and that all lions, tigers, cheetahs, bobcats, house cats, etc., are part of a taxonomic family (Felidae) – like with plants, there are some similarities within the cat family, you can see those diverse cats are certainly related, but there are lots of differences, too!

Below I'll briefly outline some of the different amaranth species under the three categories of grain amaranths, vegetable amaranths, and ornamental amaranths. Keep in mind that the leaves of grain amaranths can be eaten as vegetables (best to cook them first), and that most grain amaranths are also ornamental in appearance, so these groupings are all relative.

Grain types

There are three main species of grain amaranths. In the U.S., we grow either *Amaranthus hypochondriacus* or *Amaranthus cruentus* (from here on I'll normally shorten *Amaranthus* to the letter *A.*, unless there's a reason to spell it out). The third member of the grain amaranth species is *A. caudatus,* which is less frequently used as a grain crop. In Chapter 6 on amaranth history, I'll provide more information on how these various species were domesticated for food use by humans. For now, I'll just observe that all three grain species originated in the Americas, primarily Central and South America. Some modern amaranth grain varieties are derived from crosses of two or more species.

Compared to the vegetable and ornamental types, the grain amaranths are taller, more vigorous (produce more total biomass), have a much larger inflorescence, produce more seeds per plant, and typically have pale-colored seed (but not always). Usually vegetable and ornamental types of amaranth have black seed. The grain amaranths typically have colorful inflorescences and some varieties may show some purple or reddish coloring on the leaves or stems, but they have not been selected for appearance alone, unlike the ornamental types.

Vegetable types

Whereas the grain amaranths were domesticated in the Americas,

A grain amaranth seedling shown a few weeks after emergence.

it appears that the vegetable amaranths were domesticated in multiple parts of the world, including southeast Asia. There are many different species of *Amaranthus* that have edible leaves, but the main amaranth specie used as a leafy vegetable is *A. tri-color.* At this point in time, vegetable amaranths are commonly eaten in parts of southeast Asia, Africa (especially west central Africa), some parts of the Indian subcontinent, and in the Caribbean. To a lesser extent, amaranth leaves are used in many other countries, and it seems to me that the vegetable amaranths are gradually going from being relatively unknown foods in Europe and America to starting to show up in some farmers' markets and a few restaurants here and there as part of salads, stir fry concoctions, or specific Asian recipes.

Ornamental types

Soon after amaranths were first brought to Europe, some started to be used as ornamental plants. The exact development of now classic flowers such as Love-lies-bleeding (a type of *A. caudatus*) and Joseph's coat (*A. tricolor*) are lost to history, but may have occurred through selecting or crossing amaranth biotypes from elsewhere in the world that were brought to Europe in the 16th to 18th centuries. The traditional ornamental types are fun to grow and colorful, but it is also rewarding to try some of the more colorful grain types, such as a combination of a red or yellow-leafed Joseph's Coat in the foreground and a tall grain type in the background of a flower bed.

Ornamental amaranths being grown in front of a bank in Columbia, MO.

CHAPTER 5
VARIETIES OF AMARANTH AND SEED SOURCES

I would love to be able to say that there are many improved and regionally adapted varieties of grain amaranth that are available, but that is not currently the case. Unfortunately, seed supply of grain amaranth varieties is very limited in the U.S. at this time, and there has been almost no systematic testing of the varieties currently sold on the market to see where they grow best. On the plus side, there is tremendous genetic diversity in the grain and vegetable amaranth species to work with, so a little bit of plant breeding and field testing can go a long way with this crop. In fact, progress was quickly made in earlier efforts in the U.S. to develop grain amaranth varieties.

The Rodale Research Center in Pennsylvania (now called the Rodale Institute) released several varieties in the 1980s for farmers and researchers to evaluate in different regions of the country. The one that gained the most use was RRC343. That cultivar was later improved by David Baltensperger at the University of Nebraska and released as Plainsman in 1992. It became the standard grain amaranth variety grown in the U.S. during the 1990s and into the early 2000s. It is a good yielding variety and does well in the High Plains, such as western Nebraska, but I had lodging problems with it and most other Rodale lines under Missouri conditions. Lodging refers to a plant falling over before harvest, either because the roots give way and the whole plant falls over (this was the usual problem with the Rodale/Plainsman lines in Missouri) or the stem breaks (sometimes this happened under high winds). As of the time of this writing, Plainsman amaranth is still available through University of Nebraska Husker Genetics on a limited basis (huskergenetics.unl.edu). Garden seed packets of Plainsman are advertised through Southern Exposure Seed Exchange (see following list of seed sources).

To better address the issue of lodging and to select for other desirable characteristics, I began a process of breeding some improved amaranth lines several years ago. This breeding effort has been very low key, mostly involving some weekend effort in summer and fall months over a number of years. At the start of this variety development process, I had a plant breeder cooperator named Mike Bachman who worked with me to identify some good crosses of amaranth parent lines to use, and on making the crosses. After Mike moved on to another job, I then went through several years of field evaluating the segregating populations of offspring to pick the ones with the best phenotypes (traits that can be visually seen) and kept replanting those until a uniform line or variety was obtained. I've done nearly all this work in my home garden over the last decade, with some planting at the farm of Alan Weber, who has assisted in the process of evaluating the better lines.

Out of that effort and with Alan's help, we developed two new cultivars of amaranth that I think have good promise. The two new varieties are called **Crimson Glow** and **Golden Glow**, and I'm in the process of increasing the amount of seed available. There should be limited supplies of Crimson Glow available for people to try starting in 2019, and Golden Glow maybe a year later. Both seem to have improved lodging resistance, at least under Missouri conditions, and both are robust varieties that will grow at least 6 feet tall (1.8 m) under good soil conditions. Of the two, I'm partial to Crimson Glow because of the brilliant color of the flowers. By comparison, Plainsman amaranth and many of the Rodale lines have a nice maroon color, but Crimson Glow is considerably more vibrant, with a bright crimson color that is almost electric under a bright blue sky (see photos below, which perhaps don't do it full justice).

Adding to the appeal of this variety are the color changes the rest of the plant goes through as it matures. The leaves are a normal green most of the season, but as it gets into late summer, the leaves fade to a pale yellow-green, then turn bright yellow, sometimes looking golden in morning or evening sunlight. From a few feet away, the leaves are striking, with crimson leaf stalks (petioles), crimson edging around the leaves, and veins in the leaves also of crimson (see photos below). Even more dramatically, as the leaves start to drop, the entire stem turns a fiery crimson color, eventually creating an eye-catching combination of the crimson stalks topped by the crimson inflorescences. In Missouri, the plants provide a good color show for two months or more. Just on color appeal alone, I think Crimson Glow makes a good ornamental or garden plant, even though it was developed mainly for grain harvest. We've had a lot of visitors to our home say "Wow! What is that?" when they spot Crimson Glow in full bloom. It also looks great next to a patch of sunflowers.

A photo sequence over time of the Crimson Glow amaranth variety, which was developed by the author. This extremely colorful variety transitions from green leaves and crimson flowers in August (upper left) to golden leaves in September (upper right) and finally after leaves drop in late September, continues to provide brilliant color from the vibrant crimson stems and inflorescences (lower two photos). It puts on a good color show for at least 2 months while providing a decent amount of grain and having better resistance to lodging than most varieties.

While not as visually striking as Crimson Glow, the Golden Glow variety gradually turns a nice yellow or gold color at the peak of flowering, after first emerging as green flowers. Likewise, the stems gradually turn yellow as the plant drops its leaves and starts to dry down. The leaves will go pale green or somewhat yellow as they mature before dropping off. At this point I can't say with confidence which of these two varieties is higher in seed yield, but from limited evaluation on small plots I expect they are roughly comparable in yield, at least under Missouri growing conditions.

Golden Glow amaranth on the left and Crimson Glow variety on the right.

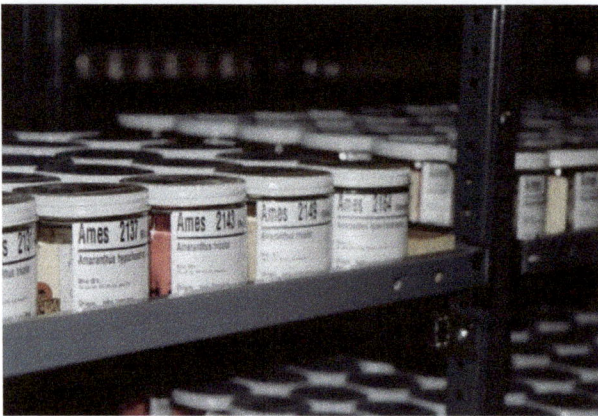

Amaranth accessions stored at the Plant Introduction Station in Ames, IA.

Other amaranth breeding efforts in the U.S.

Iowa. One of the true champions of amaranth in the United States, and even worldwide, is David Brenner. I've known David for almost 30 years, and during that time period, he has invested more sustained effort in the grain amaranths than anyone else I know. During most of that time he has worked as a plant germplasm curator with the USDA National Plant Germplasm System (NPGS), based at the North Central Plant Introduction Station affiliated with Iowa State University. Part of David's job with NPGS is to serve as the curator of amaranth germplasm, along with other crops he curates. In the case of amaranth, seeds are the germplasm that is stored, evaluated, reproduced, and distributed to researchers. David manages a collection of thousands of different types of amaranth, called accessions, from all over the world. An accession is the basic unit of what is stored in a seed bank, and can represent a variety, a mixed population of seed, or simply a group of seed or other reproducible plant part collected in a particular location. A number of the accessions are ones he personally found on plant collecting trips.

In addition to his job of evaluating, reproducing, cleaning, storing, and documenting amaranth accessions, David also distributes seeds to researchers around the world. He has been the unofficial hub of an ongoing communication network of amaranth workers around the world. He's also taken on a number of volunteer roles to advance amaranth, serving multiple times as president of the all-volunteer non-profit Amaranth Institute, hosting international conferences on amaranth, and generally doing what he can to share information on the crop. He has also done some very important work to create better opportunities for breeding amaranth going forward, in part by identifying amaranth biotypes with potentially valuable characteristics. For example, he's identified and selected for semi-dwarf types of amaranth, which could be easier to harvest, and high biomass amaranth types that have good potential as livestock forage (food). One of his key findings has been developing a type of amaranth that has a non-shattering trait, meaning that the seed will be less likely to fall off before harvest. More breeding and varietal development efforts are needed to build upon his work, but he has done a tremendous amount to enhance the future prospects of amaranth, more than anyone else I know. If you ever get to meet David, shake his hand and thank him for all he's done!

Montana. Following on the heels of the amaranth breeding by staff at the Rodale Research Center in Pennsylvania was an effort to develop varieties suited more to the Northern Plains region. I don't know the full history at Montana State University on amaranth breeding, but the two key players were Gil Stallknecht and Jurgen Schaeffer. They and their colleagues released varieties such as Monci, Amont, MT-3, and MT-5. Although none of these are currently available for sale, at least some of these are still maintained as part of the large amaranth seed collection of the National Plant Germplasm System (NPGS) run by USDA-ARS at Iowa State University (researchers can get small quantities of seed from NPGS for developing new varieties or other research work, but due to cost and limited staff resources, the seed is not available to the general public).

Tennessee. A recent breeding effort in the U.S. has gotten underway at Tennessee State University through the efforts of Matthew Blair. Starting in about 2014, he began to make crosses for improved amaranth varieties. While any breeding effort takes several years to come to fruition in terms of release of new varieties, I'm looking forward to seeing what comes out of his program.

Currently available varieties

Before I start listing varieties, some caveats: First, most of the varieties listed are priced and sold in quantities appropriate for home gardeners or small acreage growers, and are not practically priced for planting in a 40-acre field. I'm hopeful we can get back to having a commercial supply of amaranth farm seed in the near future. Second, seed sold through gardening catalogs sometimes appears under more than one name, and some appear to be landraces that are more of a mixture of similar plants than a single true variety where every plant is identical. Third, the varieties available at the time of this writing may not be available in subsequent years. Fourth, I'm only going to list varieties available in the U.S., which may or may not be available elsewhere in the world or may be sold under different names. And fifth, my listing of amaranths below is focused on the grain types of amaranths, and although I'll list a few vegetable and ornamental varieties, please be aware that many flower companies sell the ornamental amaranths under common names such as Joseph's coat and Loves-lies-bleeding, so I don't attempt to list all the possible ornamental or even vegetable amaranth sources.

I'm listing information below on varieties available as of early 2018 under the names of the companies or organizations selling them. Rather than providing a website URL that may be changed, I'll just suggest you do an internet search for the name

A tremendous diversity of plant types and flower colors is available in the grain amaranth germplasm, giving breeders plenty of material to work with in improving the crop. However, very little plant breeding is being done at this time.

of the organization, and it should quickly pop up for you, then type amaranth into the company's search box of their webpage. Most of these companies have nice photos of the different varieties on their websites.

Johnny's Selected Seeds

This worker-owned company caters to both home gardeners and small acreage commercial growers and has both organic and conventional seed. They also have one of the widest ranges of seed of any company, with a tremendous number of vegetable varieties, as well as a good selection of ornamentals, cover crops, and even some grains. Unlike many garden seed companies that only offer garden seed packets with small quantities of seed, from Johnny's you can buy larger increments for many types of seed. While they don't currently offer any of the *Amaranthus hypochondriacus* grain types of amaranth, they do offer:

Red Spike (*A. cruentus*) – Described as the darkest red flowers in their trials
Hot Biscuits (*A. cruentus)* – Described as having bronze blooms and a branching structure (meaning it is probably a wild type selection compared to cultivated types with a single stem)
Coral Fountain (*A. caudatus*) – A love-lies-bleeding type ornamental with coral pink flowers
Emerald Tassels (*A. caudatus*) – A love-lies-bleeding type ornamental with green flowers
Loves-lies-bleeding (*A. caudatus*) – The generic love-lies-bleeding type ornamental with reddish maroon flowers
Red Garnet (*A. tricolor)* – Sold primarily for sprouts but can be grown into full-sized plants with red leaves

Baker Creek Heirloom Seed

As their name implies, this seed company has focused on heirloom (older) varieties of seed that might otherwise be lost to history. This company was started in southern Missouri by Jere Gettle in the late 1990s at the age of 17. He's done a commendable job over the years of steadily growing the company and preserving a great diversity of seeds from many sources, to the benefit of gardeners and farmers everywhere. Baker Creek has one of the largest number of amaranth varieties that I've come across from a U.S.-based seed company. Their catalog descriptions are included below, in some cases abbreviated for length.

Golden Giant – Attractive golden-colored flower heads produce up to 1 lb of white seed per plant, making this a very heavy producer

Hopi Red Dye – Originally grown as a dye plant by the southwestern Hopi Nation, this variety has the reddest seedlings of any amaranth known, making it a natural for micro-green mixes. The Hopis use the deep-red flower bract as a natural dye to color their world-renowned piki bread.

Opopeo – Beautiful, large, red, upright flower spikes and bronze-green foliage make this Mexican heirloom a real knockout

Orange Giant – Ornamental 6- to 8-foot tall plants produce giant, golden orange heads, with the stems golden as well

Red Garnett – Attractive flowers and red leaves make this amaranth not only edible, but beautiful as well. Young leaves can be used for greens, or let go to seed and harvest for grain.

Pygmy Torch – Amazing dwarf amaranth variety offers all the style and brilliant color of ornamental amaranth, but at a reasonable size, reaching only to about 3 feet in height, making them perfect for smaller gardens or containers

Elena's Rojo – Red-flowering amaranth from Guatemala. This variety, like Juana's and Aurelia's listed below, has been revived in the Mayan communities of Baja Verapaz after almost being lost during their civil war; each variety is named after the woman whose family revived and saved seeds of this amaranth.

Aurelia's Verde – Native amaranth from Guatemala that flowers light green, primarily used for grain

Juana's Orange – A lovely orange variety from Guatemala, primarily used for grain

Green Calaloo – A popular green vegetable in many countries, including many islands of the Caribbean where this plant is famous for Calaloo Seafood Soup. Light green leaves are great in stews, stir-fries, and soups, having a tangy, spinach-like flavor.

Tricolor Aurora Yellow – 2-5 feet tall. Stunning contrast between the dark green lower leaves and the flower-like upper leaves—looking for all the world like oversized, yellow poinsettia flowers.

Elephant Head – This heirloom was brought to the USA from Germany in the 1880s and is so named because the huge flower heads often take on the appearance of an elephant's trunk. The 3- to 5-foot plants produce flowers that are deep reddish-purple in color. (Author's note: Though the catalog lists Germany as the source of this selection, originally these biotypes likely would have come from the Americas).

Dreadlocks – A fountain of eye-catching magenta-burgundy blooms! Here's a different amaranth—curious flower-heads in a weeping habit, with "tassels" sometimes reaching to the ground. Plants seldom exceed 3-foot height. A form of love-lies-bleeding.

Loves-lies-bleeding – they have both the red and green flowered types of love-lies-bleeding.

Native Seeds/SEARCH

This non-profit organization focuses on saving heirloom seeds from the southwestern U.S. and northern Mexico. Based in Arizona, they not only test different seed collections in field trials but also grow out seed for sale to gardeners to help preserve a rich diversity of plants appropriate to dry growing regions. Like Baker Creek, they have one of the largest number of amaranth varieties. Their catalog descriptions are included below, in some cases abbreviated for length:

Alamos – A beautiful amaranth from the colonial town of Alamos in southern Sonora, Mexico. The leaves are green with red-tinged veins and the "flowers" (bracts) are bright fuchsia-colored.

Alegria – *A. cruentus.* Produces blond seed typically used for the traditional central Mexican confection, alegria, which is made with popped seeds and honey. Occasional black seeds.

Guarijio Grain – *A. hypochondriachus x A. hybridus.* "Guegui." From the Rio Mayo in Sonora, Mexico, a white-seeded grain used for tamales, pinole (a traditional Mexican drink) or popping. Try popping the grain over a dry, hot pan and add to granola, fruit salads, or mix with honey to make traditional Mexican alegria. Inflorescences range from light yellow-green to pink to fuchsia.

Guatemalan – Originally collected in San Martin Jilotepeque, Guatemala. The leaves are green as are the "flowers" (bracts), though occasional red inflorescences are also produced. Seeds are blond.

Hopi Red Dye – *A. cruentus.* "Komo". The beautiful plant can grow 6 feet tall with long and dark reddish green leaves. Young tender leaves are excellent in salads and add a bright pinkish red accent. The black seeds are also edible. The Hopi make a scarlet natural food dye to color piki bread. This variety readily crosses with wild *Amaranthus powellii.* Originally collected in Lower Moenkopi.

Mano de Obispo – *Celosia cristata.* Bishop's Hand. This ornamental cockscomb decorates graves for Dia de los Muertos (All Souls Day). Flowers are magenta, some golden. Plants reach up to 3 feet in height. The black seed is edible. (Author's note – Bishop's hand is from a different genus of plants than the amaranths that are the focus of this book but it is a part of the large Amaranthaceae family)

Marbled – Originally collected in the state of Morelos, Mexico in 1979. The inflorescences are predominantly red but marbled with green. The green leaves have light red venation.

Mayo Grain – *A. cruentus.* A gorgeous amaranth from Alamos, Sonora. Bright fuchsia inflorescences and dark reddish green leaves. The leaves are used as quelites (greens). Seeds are used for esquite (parched), pinole, and atole (traditional Mexican drinks).

Mexican Grain – A blond seed produced from green plants and flowers. Original seed donated to Rodale Research by a gardener in Hobbs, New Mexico.

Moenkopi Mix – A possible cross with green leaves and inflorescences. Seeds are black. From Lower Moenkopi.

Mountain Pima Grain – From the Sonora/Chihuahua border in Mexico. The leaves are used for greens and the black seeds are ground for pinole.

New Mexico – From a dooryard garden near Rinconada, its beautiful pink and white inflorescence yield edible golden seeds.

Pauite – From a garden on the Kaibab Southern Paiute Reservation in southern Utah. Edible seeds and leaves.

Tarahumara Okute – Originally collected from a ranch above Batopilas, an old silver mining town stretched alongside the Rio Batopilas at the bottom of Barranca del Cobre. Black seeds with brilliant red flowers and stems. A showy ornamental but the seeds and young leaves can be eaten.

Southern Exposure Seed Exchange

This is a worker-run cooperative based in Virginia that focuses on seeds for the southeastern U.S. and mid-Atlantic. They offer a broad diversity of vegetables, grains, greens, and even cotton. They have a few varieties of amaranth, with abbreviated descriptions below.

Plainsman (*A. hypochondriacus*) – This variety has been the main one used on commercial farms in years past, has maroon colored flowers

Mayo Indian (*A. cruentus*) – Described as having crimson blooms with black seed

Golden amaranth – Described as having gold or gold-bronze blooms

Seeds of Change

This company started out in the late 1980s selling organic seed and later added some unique food products. Although they don't sell many varieties of amaranth they have a unique burgundy leaf one. See their descriptions below:

Burgundy – This tall, dramatic plant with long burgundy plumes bears plentiful, edible, and nutritious white seeds. Its tender young reddish-purple leaves add color to salads.
Hopi Red Dye – This heirloom produces seedlings for colorful microgreens, deep red baby leaves for salads or steaming, and flowers for bouquets.

Other seed sources for amaranth

The above list is not an all-inclusive one for companies selling amaranth. Garden seed companies such as Burpees and Park Seed carry the basic ornamental amaranths, and Eden Brothers has a nice selection of ornamental amaranths as well as the callaloo vegetable type and a couple of the grain types. Even Amazon lists some amaranth seed from a variety of seed dealers. Undoubtedly, there are other amaranth seed sources I've left out, but regardless of where you get the seed, try planting a few varieties of amaranth yourself!

CHAPTER 6
HISTORY OF AMARANTH

In the introduction to this book, I wrote about the remarkable history of amaranth connected to the arrival of Cortez and his band of Spanish conquistadors in Mexico during the early 1500s. The use of amaranth far predates the time of the Aztecs, however, so let's journey farther back in time, to when agriculture began and eventually amaranth use started in the Americas.

The more anthropologists learn about early humans, the more they realize that modern humans (*Homo sapiens*) spread around the world much earlier than was previously realized. As they spread around the globe, they lived in small bands as hunter-gatherers for many thousands of years, so for much of human history, the process of getting food depended entirely on what the land and sea could provide without cultivation; humans hunted, fished, and gathered seeds, fruit, leaves, nuts, insects, and whatever else proved edible. To better obtain food where it was seasonably available, we think that in many cases these early humans periodically picked up and moved to where food was more plentiful.

The process of agriculture began roughly 10,000 years ago, when some groups of humans became more fixed to one place. This process was probably gradual in most cases and we can only make educated guesses on how it began; perhaps they noticed that some seeds they had gathered and then accidentally spilled on the way into camp, had later started growing, giving them the idea they could purposefully plant things.

Many of the first agricultural areas, whether along the Nile River in Egypt, the Euphrates River in Mesopotamia, or the Mississippi River in America, were floodplains. Rivers, in the process of flooding, encourage growth of fast-growing annual plants that can quickly become established in recently deposited soil sediments of flood plains. Annual plants rely heavily on seeds for reproduction. The soil sediments deposited by the flooding provided fertility for seedlings of the annual plants that quickly colonized exposed floodplain sediments. Over time, since seeds are nutritionally dense and easily carried and stored, humans gravitated towards domesticating annual plants for seed harvesting (of course fruit and nut trees and bushes are a whole other matter). Annual plants are ones that grow to maturity and reproduce in a year or less.

Ethnobotanists, scientists who study the traditional use of plants by people, often look for particular cues as to when a plant was first domesticated. If they can find seeds in archaeological digs, either intact, or more likely, carbonized by being partially burned (and preserved) in a camp fire, they can study the characteristics of those seeds under a microscope. If they notice that the ancient seeds have a thinner seed coat, larger size, or other changes in shape or color versus the wild population of seeds present in that area, they will conclude that humans were purposefully growing that plant as a food crop, and over time, adapting it to better fit their needs as a crop.

Domestication of amaranth into a food crop, starting from wild plants

Although the history of amaranth is not as well studied as major crops such as maize or wheat, one man, Dr. Jonathan D. Sauer, fortunately took upon himself the rigorous task of researching the domestication of various amaranth species, first as a doctoral student in St. Louis working with Washington University and the Missouri Botanic Garden in the late 1940s, and then as a University of Wisconsin faculty member. Later in his career, he moved to UCLA, specializing in biogeography. He wrote a number of publications about amaranth, and later summarized his findings on amaranth as part of a book called the "Historical geography of crop plants," which he published at the age of 75 in 1993. The book is a fascinating narrative on the early history of many food crops we eat today. Notably, he wrote in the book's introduction, "It now appears that crop domestication has been a process, diffuse in space and time, rather than an event. Even within a single crop species, wide-ranging wild progenitors have been repeatedly domesticated at different times and different regions." In other words, he is saying there was no singular domestication event; we can't say that in the year 4257 BC in the Valley of X, such and such crop was domesticated – the process is far more complex than that. I give full credit to Dr. Sauer and his book for the following information on amaranth domestication.

The first thing Dr. Sauer pointed out on amaranth domestication is that the amaranth family (Amaranthaceae) has over 50 genera and close to 1000 species. He concentrated his work on the grain amaranths (the genus *Amaranthus)*, and that's where I will also focus my summary of their history and domestication.

Dr. Sauer commented that "*Amaranthus* includes 75 or so wild and weedy species native to tropical and temperate regions of the whole world but is most diverse in the Americas," and that potherb types of amaranths were domesticated in Asia; these were plants that had low seed yields but were grown instead for their leaves. In the Americas, although leaves were sometimes eaten, human use of *Amaranthus* species was more focused on seed (grain) harvest. Sauer observed that domesticated types of grain amaranth have seed the same size as wild-type plants of those species, but the process of human selection led to cultigens (varieties) with larger inflorescences (seed heads) and often taller stalks than the wild types. People have also selected over time for brightly colored amaranth flowering seed heads, something I've done in my own plant breeding with amaranth, developing one variety with particularly bright crimson flower colors, compared to the more typical maroon, and a second variety with golden flowers – more information on these varieties is in the preceding chapter on amaranth varieties and seed sources.

There are three species of amaranth that are considered grain amaranths: *Amaranthus hypochondriacus* (the type usually grown in the U.S.), *Amaranthus cruentus,* and *Amaranthus caudatus.* Sauer pointed out that although these three species all differ from each other in specific flowering characteristics, they are similar in having dark seeds in the wild populations and primarily light-colored seeds in the domesticated cultivars. He noted that the light-colored or pale-seeded amaranths have seed that germinates immediately, unlike wild-types where a high percentage of seed is dormant, needing time and weathering conditions before germination. He also commented that all three species are highly variable in plant and flower color, something I have noticed myself among the many genetic types of these three species.

Sauer postulated that selecting for differently colored flower types or leaf colors would have helped prehistoric farmers identify their own domesticated plants from those of the wild type, making it easier to remove the wild plants from a cultivated patch and to save seed from preferred plants. I personally think that those early farmers just naturally gravitated towards the more brightly colored amaranth types because of their beauty. After all, in other crops of Mesoamerica, like maize and beans, while seed colors varied dramatically, farmers pretty much had their choice of two colors of plant – green or green. Amaranth would have added some welcome color to their fields.

As to which of the three grain amaranth species was domesticated first, Sauer believed that honor likely belonged to *A. cruentus.* Light-colored seeds of *A. cruentus* dating from 6000 years before present (B.P), have been found in caves in the southern Mexican state of Puebla, near the city of Tehaucan; the light-coloring of the seeds is a strong clue that those seeds were from domesticated amaranth plants. However, Sauer was quick to note that the seeds found in those caves could easily have come from elsewhere in the region. He believed *A. cruentus* was developed from the wild plant *Amaranthus hybridus*, a plant that is widely distributed throughout both temperate and tropical parts of the

Americas. I find it interesting that *A. hybridus* has green flowers, unlike most domesticated amaranth grain cultivars. He also reported that pale-seeded remains of *A. cruentus* have been found throughout southern Mexico and Guatemala. It's also worth noting that the process of domestication with *A. cruentus* could have started well before 6000 years ago, but we simply don't have any earlier archaeological evidence of that at this time. Further molecular work on amaranth species will gradually provide additional insights on the domestication process.

According to Sauer, the second type of grain amaranth, *A. hypocondriacus,* first showed up "in the archaeological record at Tehaucan about 500 A.D. (2500 B.P.), as a pale-seeded cultivar probably domesticated long before and some distance away. He further indicated that "*A. hypocondriacus* is closely related to both *A. cruentus* and a wild species, *A. powellii,* and it seems likely that it is a hybrid between the two." He thought the fact that *A. powellii* is found in relatively dry areas of northern Mexico and southwestern U.S. may have imparted greater drought-tolerance into *A. hypocondriacus* compared to *A. cruentus.*

After domestication, amaranth spread into other parts of the Americas. Regarding the spread of *A. cruentus*, Sauer said that "an extremely dark red variety was grown by Pueblo peoples of Arizona and New Mexico to color ceremonial maize bread." *A. hypochondriacus* also spread into the same region, being grown by cliff-dwelling people in the southwestern U.S. This use continued to near modern times, as John Wesley Powell "received amaranth seed by trade with the Southern Paiute." This was during his exploration of the Colorado River through the southwestern U.S. in 1872-73. I was excited to learn that fact since John Wesley Powell was the brother-in-law of my great, great, great uncle John Davis, a former U.S. Congressman.

Migrating even farther away from Mexico, according to Sauer, "caches of *A. hypochondriacus* have also been found in Ozark rock shelters and dated at about 1100 A.D." However, we don't know whether amaranth was actually grown in the Ozarks of Missouri and Arkansas or ended up there through trade. Given that I've been able to grow amaranth quite well in Missouri, it certainly is conceivable that it was grown in the Ozarks a millennium or more ago.

As to the third of the three amaranth grain species, *A. caudatus,* Sauer indicated the origin is less understood. He believed *A. caudatus* likely develop by hybridization between *A. cruentus* and wild species, as *A. cruentus* was traded and grown down into South America. Eventually, *A. caudatus* was routinely grown "in the temperate Andean [mountain] valleys of Peru, Bolivia, and northwestern Argentina," according to Sauer.

Use of amaranth by Aztecs and other American cultures

If someone just got their history from cereal boxes, especially amaranth breakfast cereal, they might assume that amaranth was grown only by Aztecs. Although we know more about their use of amaranth than any earlier American civilization, there is little doubt that other major cultures of the Americas used amaranth. A thousand years before the Aztec civilization reached its zenith, Teotihuacan was the thriving center of a regional economy and culture. Given that Teotihuacan, with its great pyramids, was only about a two-day walk from the later capitol of the Aztecs (present day Mexico City), it's highly likely that amaranth was used by the Teotihuacan people. Other early American civilizations such as the Olmec and Maya may have used amaranth, but being primarily located at lower elevations, their use of it may have been less extensive. The Incans, as contemporaries of the Aztecs, appear to have used at least a modest amount of grain amaranth, along with a considerable amount of quinoa, a grain with many similar nutritional characteristics to amaranth. The Incans grew amaranth and called it "kiwicha," using it in some parts of the Andes Mountains of South America, where grain amaranth is still grown today.

Amaranth spread in post-Columbian times

While early European explorers of the New World searched for gold and other treasures, one of the things they brought back of more lasting influence was seeds. These seeds, including amaranths, quickly spread hand-to-hand along trade routes. Initially, it appears that the colorful grain amaranths were usually planted as an ornamental. All three species showed up in European references soon after the Spanish arrival in Central and South America. By the time European explorers such as Livingstone arrived in remote parts of Africa, amaranth had already beaten them there. Sauer stated that a type of *A. cruentus* with dark red plant color and dark seeds was the one most often found in Africa and spread throughout Europe. He noted that the pale seeded type of *A. cruentus* did not show up in European historical records, nor was that species of amaranth grown as a grain in Europe.

Sauer's comments on the spread of *A. hypochondriacus* are quite interesting, and are worth quoting intact:

> *A. hypochondriacus,* by contrast [to *A. cruentus*] was introduced to the Old World in both dark and pale seed forms and in a wide variety of plant color forms. In Europe, the species was not used for grain, and dark seed forms gradually replaced the pale seed forms; the latter are present in European grown specimens from the 16th until the mid-19th century. By then, the pale seed forms had been taken on to Asia to become a grain crop. The earliest records of the crop there are from the 18th century in Ceylon and South India, where it became a staple of the hill tribes. During the 19th century, it became widespread in India, most importantly in the Himalaya, and across the interior of China to eastern Siberia. The grain is used much as in Mexico, parched, popped, milled for tortilla-like chapatis. It is also used in peculiar Asian recipes. In India especially, it has acquired ceremonial importance for certain festivals. An outpost of the crop was established in

East Africa during World War II to supply the local Indian communities when the supplies of the grain from India were interrupted. Several hundred hectares a year were [still] grown in Kenya in the 1980s.

Regarding *A. caudatus,* Sauer stated "the species is clearly recognizable in Flemish, Swiss, and English botanical literature of the early 17th century, attributed to both Peru and Asia." He points out the ornamental type of *A. caudatus* we now call "love-lies-bleeding" became popular in European gardens, and of course remains popular worldwide today. Sauer notes, however, that the drooping flower panicle form of love-lies-bleeding is just one of many flowering types of *A. caudatus* that can be found in the Andean Mountains of South America.

One of the agricultural tragedies of history, seemingly caused by the ignorance of Spanish conquistadors, is that amaranth largely disappeared from it's original home in Mexico and other parts of Latin America. Had the Spaniards supported the use of amaranth in the way they supported the use of corn, we'd likely see millions of acres of amaranth grown around the world today, and it would probably still be a prominent crop in Mexico, rather than one that is slowly being resurrected in that region.

Amaranth in recent decades

Although many people have contributed to amaranth's modern progress, one person's efforts particularly stand out. In the 1970s, Robert "Bob" Rodale became interested in amaranth as a great source of nutrition for hungry people around the world. Fortunately, as the head of a successful magazine and book publishing empire, Rodale Press, he had the financial resources and publicity platform to do something about it. In 1976, he started the Rodale Research Farm near Emmaus, Pennsylvania, to carry out work on organic agriculture and alternative forms of farming, including research on amaranth. Over time, with his encouragement and financial support, the Rodale Research Center staff developed a dozen or so new varieties of amaranth, worked out some of the production methods, evaluated its nutrition, and tested it in food products, developing new recipes. The varieties they developed were the first modern varieties developed for North America, and were the first widely distributed varieties for temperate regions worldwide. Through Rodale Press, particularly the highly popular Organic Gardening magazine, Bob Rodale encouraged people to try eating amaranth and even grow some in their garden.

By the mid-1980s, almost a decade after Bob Rodale became an advocate for amaranth, and not long after the first Rodale varieties were released, U.S. farmers were starting to grow amaranth. I believe Rodale's publicity and work on amaranth also created a surge in interest internationally in amaranth, for it was around the mid-1980s that it started to be researched more in other countries and tried on a wider range of farms.

Tragically, Bob Rodale was killed at the age of 60 in an auto accident while promoting regenerative agriculture in Russia in 1990. With the loss of his passion and diminishing financial resources, the Rodale Research Center soon had to drop its amaranth program to focus on other aspects of organic farming. While the center, now called the Rodale Institute, has continued to do good work over the years on a limited budget, I've sometimes wondered how much farther amaranth would have gotten had Bob lived longer. I only crossed paths with him once, hearing him give a presentation on regenerative farming in about 1986, but from what I've read, he was ahead of his time on many things, including ideas like soil health.

Still, Bob Rodale's impact lingered on. By the early 1990s, there were reports of amaranth being used in China, likely using varieties developed by the Rodale Research Center, and amaranth was starting to get more recognition in Mexico again. Although I don't know the full history of amaranth over time in Mexico, I do know that a major driving force for re-establishing amaranth in its ancestral home of Mexico was the dedicated work of people involved with Puente a la Salud Comunitaria. This small but impactful non-profit was started in the southern Mexican state of Oaxaca in 2003 by Katherine Lorenz and Kate Seely. The story of some of their work is told in Chapter 8, and to me it's a real example of what a modest financial investment can do if channeled through a committed and focused group of people working to improve the lives of others.

Other aspects of amaranth's recent use in the last few decades, including where it's recently been grown, are described in more depth in Chapter 7 on where amaranth is grown today. Suffice it to say that the history of amaranth continues to be written. I hope that some of you reading this book will do your own part, whether small or large, to help amaranth keep moving forward as a crop that can beautify our gardens and fields and provide nutritious food for many people.

CHAPTER 7

WHERE AMARANTH IS GROWN IN THE WORLD TODAY AND PROSPECTS FOR EXPANSION

As described in the previous chapter on amaranth history, amaranth was first developed as a crop in Mexico. Use of amaranth spread out from Mexico, not in a smooth, linear process, but by fits and starts, depending on the interests of plant explorers, researchers, gardeners, and farmers. Like with many crops, amaranth has sometimes had an initial burst of interest in a country, then faded to a much lower level of use. Although there is no governmental effort to systematically collect data on amaranth production in the world today, some information on where there is current or recent amaranth production comes from interpersonal communications between amaranth workers around the world.

This chapter provides a brief overview of grain amaranth production and prospects, first in the United States, then Mexico, and then other parts of the world. It includes a brief summary of vegetable amaranth growing regions, and ends with the outlook for additional areas where amaranth could be grown in the future.

Grain amaranth production and prospects in the United States

Grain amaranth has been grown in several parts of the U.S., most principally the High Plains region. In the late 1980s and early 1990s, there was a bit of a push to get farmers lined up to grow amaranth in the High Plains of western Nebraska, eastern Colorado, and some in Montana. Perhaps 50 or more farmers gave amaranth a try in those growing areas, while it was also being evaluated by farmers in a few other locations, such as southern Minnesota, Iowa, North Dakota, and later Missouri. Due to lack of stable marketing options and long distances for delivery, as well as the unfamiliarity of the crop, many farmers who tried it gave up after a year or two. A few farmers persisted in growing amaranth for over a decade, such as Phil Sanders in Nebraska and Arris Sigle in Kansas. Unfortunately, the lack of markets and profitability, especially when corn and soybean prices surged starting in 2007, ultimately led nearly all of these farmers to give up the crop.

At its peak, perhaps in the late 1980s or early 1990s, grain amaranth was probably grown on 50 to 100 farms in any one year with a total of perhaps 5,000 to 10,000 acres in the U.S. As of 2018, there is very little grain amaranth grown in the U.S., especially for commercial purposes. Nearly all of it used in the U.S. is imported from other countries.

There has been enough experience with grain amaranth in the U.S. to show it is widely adaptable, from the more humid, higher rainfall areas of the eastern U.S. to the more arid western Plains. It was grown for many years with success in southeastern Pennsylvania at the Rodale Research Center and on a few farms in that area. I myself grew it in my garden in Maryland on the outskirts of Washington, DC, for three years in the mid-1990s, and it grew well. In Missouri, a climate similar to Maryland, in over 25 years of field and small plot trials, I've found it generally does well, whether the summer is wet or dry. Even though there have been so few varieties to work with, there has been success growing it over a broad north-south axis, from northern areas such as Montana, North Dakota, and Minnesota (and Canada), down to more southern areas such as southeast Missouri and Tennessee. I think it's fair to say that amaranth is more adaptable than most grain crops to a wide range of conditions.

The primary limitation holding back amaranth in the U.S. has been creating a coordinated system between growers and buyers. Too often, the individuals who bought amaranth, especially in the 1980s and 1990s, were only in business for a short period, either as brokers or in a couple of cases had set up very small scale processing facilities. Larger food companies have made some limited use of grain amaranth as a flour ingredient in breads and other products (see Chapter 3), but they are not interested in contracting directly with farmers and just want to buy amaranth in bulk. I base the preceding comment on two revealing conversations I had with large food companies about amaranth. The first was a meeting with some senior food ingredient buyers from Ralston Purina out of St. Louis in the early 1990s, and then later I had a similar discussion with a senior vice-president at General Mills in Minneapolis in the early 2000s.

The corporate managers I spoke to in both cases were well aware of grain amaranth, and somewhat surprisingly, both companies had done research on use of grain amaranth flour in their test kitchens. Both companies were intrigued with amaranth's nutritional characteristics and felt it had good functionality for use in food products. However, both were holding back from putting amaranth into their products for two key reasons, one being the relatively high price of the grain, and even more importantly, because of the perceived lack of a ready supply for them to purchase on short notice. I asked the people I spoke with about the possibility of their companies directly working with growers to offer contracts for amaranth production. While sympathetic to farmers, and recognizing the potential value of such a direct connection, at the time that was not something their companies were interested in or even set up to do. What they really wanted, as food company business managers, was to know that there was a decent-sized warehouse somewhere in the U.S. with a constant and ready supply of food-grade processed amaranth flour, especially at a reasonable price. If that was available, they indicated they would have been more than happy to put amaranth into some of their products.

Among people who have worked on new or alternative crops, this disconnect between production and demand, between farmers and buyers/processors, is considered a "Catch-22." The farmers won't grow the crop because they don't see a market, and the food companies won't use the product because it hasn't already been produced and put in a warehouse for their quick access. What is needed is an effort to bridge the gap, either through public and/or private sector investment, so that farmers can receive a guaranteed contract that they will get paid for growing the crop, and a reasonable supply of grain can be built up for the food marketplace to tap into. This has happened with other crops over time. It happened when A.E. Staley made a commitment to buying a Chinese crop called soybeans in central Illinois in the 1920s (soybeans were relatively unknown in the U.S. at that time), and more recently it happened with canola in Canada, followed by later adoption of canola in the U.S. and other countries. Other crops have followed a similar path to prominence.

More domestic amaranth production is needed to interest larger food buyers, who want to have a ready supply of the grain to access.

To the extent there has been some modest success with amaranth in the U.S., it's been because of the efforts of a few smaller companies, perhaps most notably Nu-World Foods (formerly Nu-World Amaranth). Nu-World Foods is a family-owned and operated company started by a food industry consultant, Larry Walters, and his engineering brother, Terry Walters. Now the next generation, Larry's children Susan and Jonathan, are running the company, based out of Naperville, IL. The company had a few hurdles in early years due to a volatile marketplace for amaranth, but has succeeded in recent years by expanding into other grains in addition to amaranth, while continuing to offer amaranth products. However, they, like other U.S. food companies, have found that nearly all their recent amaranth supply has had to come from imported product.

Going forward, I am hopeful that at some point an enterprising group of people will find a good niche for where amaranth can be grown and processed profitably, and start to build a mid-sized business around the crop, perhaps in combination with other grains. Most likely, that production region will be in the Great Plains, where amaranth can compete as a drought tolerant crop. However, it is possible to imagine it could also occur elsewhere in the United States, particularly if consumer demand for locally-grown foods extended to locally-grown grains.

Grain amaranth production and prospects in Mexico

As the historical home for amaranth, one would think that Mexico would still be a major growing area for the crop. However, as noted in the previous chapter on amaranth history, the Spanish conquistadors seem to have made an effort to eliminate or greatly reduce amaranth production in the 1500s, and thereafter it almost disappeared from Mexican use. Thankfully, some Mexican farmers kept alive the tradition of growing amaranth, and in recent decades, it has started a slow climb back from near oblivion to where it is now a viable crop for farmers in some parts of Mexico, though still a minor one overall.

A number of people, ranging from farmers to university, agency, and NGO workers, have worked to bring amaranth back to being a viable crop over the last few decades. Probably the most dedicated and sustained effort has come from a small non-profit called Puente a la Salud Comunitaria, and their efforts and progress are the subject of the chapter following this one. In brief, as of 2018, they were working with close to 300 farm families in the southern Mexico state of Oaxaca on amaranth production, and had also succeeded in helping spur interest in amaranth in other parts of Mexico. The amaranth grown in Mexico is used by the families that grow it both as an important source of nutrition for those families, and also as a potential income crop that can be sold in their region or possibly exported.

There is great potential for further expansion of amaranth in Mexico. It provides a beneficial nutrition complement to maize as a food source, particularly where beans or other protein-rich foods may be in limited supply. It also has great potential to be sold into urban centers in Mexico and exported to the United States and/or other countries where demand for nutritious food grains is high, and consumers are willing to pay a premium price. There is a large amount of amaranth germplasm adapted to Mexico, although additional public/private sector investments in breeding improved amaranths for Mexico are needed, just like in other parts of the world.

Grain amaranth production and prospects in other parts of the world

It's hard to find good information about the extent of amaranth production in places outside of Mexico and the U.S. Some of what I know comes from periodic amaranth conferences held by the non-profit Amaranth Institute (an all-volunteer association of university, non-profit, agency, food company, and farmers based out of the U.S. but with international members). At those small but important conferences, a number of countries have been represented over the years. What I can do is identify places where some work has been done internationally with amaranth, but my reporting here is based on limited information that probably doesn't come close to reflecting the full picture of amaranth in the world today.

Going back a century or more, one of the first places outside the Americas to have some fields of grain amaranth was the Indian subcontinent, with reports from travelers of seeing fields of amaranth in Nepal and mountainous areas of northern India. The fact that amaranth can tolerate heat but also high elevations may be a reason it made its way to that mountainous region fairly early on. My impression is that much of the grain amaranth sold in the U.S. today is currently coming from India, which would imply that they are the low cost producers in the current world market for amaranth and are able to supply at least moderate quantities.

In more recent decades, China and parts of sub-Saharan Africa have been some of the more active areas for amaranth investigation and production. At one amaranth conference in the early 2000s, a conference attendee from China reported that he believed there was as much as 100,000 acres (40,000 hectares) of grain amaranth in China. However, I have not seen that acreage figure substantiated elsewhere and don't know what the current trend of amaranth in China is. I have heard from more than one source that a typical use of grain amaranth in China was as a "green chop" forage to feed to the family pig. This makes some sense, as amaranth is after all a member of the pigweed family! What I have been told is that some small-scale farmers in China would grow a small plot of amaranth, and after it reached a certain size, cut a small number of plants each day to feed the family hog(s). It was fed as a whole green plant, with or without seeds, and no further processing done to it. As of the early 2000s, there was some belief that the grain amaranth grown in China may have been primarily a variety developed in the U.S. There are certainly parts of China that have similar growing conditions to the Midwestern U.S., so I'm sure that U.S.-developed amaranth varieties would perform adequately in China.

We've been fortunate to have a number of amaranth workers from Africa attend the U.S.-based amaranth conferences and report on their work, so that gives me a better feel for what is happening there than in India or China. Some of the work on amaranth in Africa has been led through government funded agriculture research efforts, but my impression (perhaps inaccurate), is that the majority of amaranth work there has been brought about by international non-profit organizations working on hunger and nutrition programs, typically food-relief religious organizations.

Kenya, Tanzania, and Uganda are east-central African countries where multi-year projects have been pursued to teach farmers about both growing and using grain amaranth. Probably the first reports I heard in the early 1990s of work with amaranth in Africa were from Kenya, but I believe some amaranth work goes back further in time than that in Africa. Certainly vegetable use of amaranth in parts of west-central Africa appears to date back much further, likely to the 1800s.

As in southern Mexico, there are parts of east-central Africa where calorie consumption is adequate but malnutrition is present due to a heavy reliance on a maize-based diet. Maize (corn) is native to Mexico, but was introduced to Africa by Europeans and unfortunately had a major impact in displacing some of the more nutritious native food grains such as pearl millet and cowpeas. Amaranth provides one possible solution to those that are malnourished, by boosting not only total protein content but also by providing a protein source that is well-balanced in amino acid profile, unlike maize. Amaranth is also high in iron and vitamin A, nutrients that maize is low in, and is somewhat higher in fat and zinc, which also help overcome malnutrition.

Of course, since amaranth is a non-familiar food in most African communities where it has been introduced, there is a fair amount of effort needed to educate family members on how to use amaranth and why they should consider using it. Some of the international relief workers and their African partners I have met have been effective in their community education efforts. Unfortunately, such projects are sometimes of short duration due to funding restrictions or personnel changes, and then the interest starts to fade away in a given region. This is a key challenge of international agriculture development, to do investment in a long-term fashion and to take a systems-based approach to understanding what the barriers are to adoption of a new food source, even one as nutritious as amaranth.

Prospects for further expansion of amaranth in Africa are variable, depending on the local growing conditions, competition from other crops and food sources, grain processing and storage, and even political instability in some areas. If more of the major international investors in Africa, such as World Bank, U.S. AID, or private foundations such as the Bill and Melinda Gates Foundation, would take more interest in amaranth, then more rapid progress could be made. I hope this greater level of investment will happen, given both the malnutrition that exists in many parts of Africa and the greater stress that climate change will place on growing nutritious food in many regions.

Vegetable amaranth growing regions

I am less familiar with the worldwide use of vegetable amaranths than grain amaranths, but felt it important to at least provide some information on the significant role of the vegetable amaranth species. The first use of amaranth as a vegetable likely started in the same areas where amaranth was harvested for grain, as the grain types have leaves that are quite edible, if not always the best tasting. As plant seeds were traded around the world in the 1800s, amaranth started to find it's way into kitchen gardens in scattered parts of the world. At some point in the 1800s, amaranth began to be used as a potherb or vegetable in Africa, particularly west central Africa. Slaves brought to the Caribbean region from west central Africa sometimes brought a few of their food traditions with them, so eventually amaranth as a vegetable started to show up in the Caribbean region as well.

My understanding is that vegetable amaranths are particularly popular as a chopped and steamed vegetable side-dish in Caribbean countries like Jamaica, where it is called "callaloo." Spices are added to the chopped amaranth leaves, and sometimes other vegetables. Also, the leaves are sometimes boiled or used as a stew ingredient. The fact that vegetable amaranth varieties range from dark green to an intense maroon color helps with their visual appeal, and the high nutrition content of the leaves, similar to spinach or kale, is leading to expanded interest. In fact, vegetable amaranths are starting to show up at some farmers' market stands in the U.S. and are being sold by garden seed companies.

Vegetable amaranths are also used in parts of southeast Asia. I've had a hard time finding much information on the extent of use there or the timing of when this developed. However, the growing popularity of Asian vegetables and foods in the western world is also bringing new attention to vegetable amaranths in the U.S.

Future areas of adoption for grain amaranth

When I think about the next 50 to 100 years of food production on our good green Earth, I passionately believe that we will need a more diversified base of food crops, including grains, to deal with a changing climate and growing population. I address this theme in more depth in my epilogue for the book, but for purposes of this chapter, wanted to identify possible areas where such expanded use of amaranth could take place.

Based on what I've seen and experienced with amaranth in the U.S., as well as reports on its production elsewhere in the world, there's no question that amaranth is one of the most widely adapted food grains we have available to us. We still have a lot to learn about where the best locations to grow amaranth, but in short, it will grow at high and low elevation (one of the few crops to do that), in humid or dry regions, and on a variety of soil types. It's an undemanding crop from the standpoint of needing fertilizers or irrigation, and can be grown and harvested by hand without expensive machinery. On the negative side, it does require more work to harvest by hand than corn (but not more than wheat or oats), and it does have a fair number of insect pests. Another restriction is that current varieties are not nearly as high yielding as most of the more popular grains and oilseeds, which reflects in large part the lack of modern plant breeding with the crop.

There is tremendous genetic diversity available with amaranth, making it possible that funding investments in plant breeding could lead to higher yielding varieties particularly adapted to various growing regions of the world. Compared to many of the crops I've worked with, the amount of genetic variation in amaranth is remarkable, and more than one economic species is available to us, increasing the amount of genetic material to work with.

If I had to speculate, I'd guess that the geographic regions where amaranth is most likely to advance are areas where maize is the predominate crop and thus there is a shortage of protein, and also in areas where wheat is grown because of those being low-moisture temperate regions where amaranth is well-adapted. In much of the moisture-limited wheat regions, I think amaranth will typically be grown as a non-irrigated crop, though there will be some exceptions where it is irrigated. We may also see it grown in a niche way where there is strong demand for locally-produced foods and people looking for high nutrition, such as in areas where people have more disposable income for food purchases.

CHAPTER 8

A REMARKABLE SUCCESS STORY WITH AMARANTH

The story of Puente a la Salud Comunitaria,
a non-profit working with farmers and rural villagers in southern
Mexico[1]

Katherine Lorenz and Pete Noll

Addressing rural health needs in Southern Mexico led to an amaranth-based organization

By Katherine Lorenz[2]

In the spring and summer of 2003, I found myself driving around through the deserts and mountains of southern Mexico in a VW Bug with another young American, Kate Seely. We had the little car loaded to the brim with bags of popped amaranth for villagers to try using, small seed packets of amaranth for planting in gardens, and some literature with lots of photos on how to cook and eat amaranth. We traveled from one rural village to another in the state of Oaxaca, Mexico, meeting with women and men, trying to spread the word about amaranth. It was kind of ironic,

---

1 *Introductory note by Rob Myers. The best success story I have come across over the years on amaranth's impact has been the work of a small non-profit working in Oaxaca, Mexico, called Puente a la Salud Comunitaria (www.puentemexico.org). I first met one of the co-founders, Katherine Lorenz, at an Amaranth Institute meeting not long after she began working with amaranth in Mexico, and got better acquainted with her over the years, along with her successor, Pete Noll, the current executive director of Puente. They and their colleagues have done a great deal to not only advance amaranth in Mexico, but also to help many rural people in southern Mexico with their health, income, and general well-being. Their story deserves to be told. While Katherine no longer works at Puente, she remains involved with the organization on their board of directors. She shares here the story of the early days of Puente and some of the challenges addressed by the organization, and then Pete picks up the Puente story starting in 2009. Thanks to Pete for the photos included in this chapter.*

2 *Katherine Lorenz was a co-founder of Puente a la Salud Comunitaria with Kate Seely in 2003 and later served as executive director of the organization until 2008. She currently serves as President of the Cynthia and George Mitchell Foundation, and has served in a number of other leadership roles with philanthropic organizations.*

because here we were in Mexico, one of the home regions for amaranth from centuries ago, and yet the crop had been almost forgotten in the villages we were visiting.

One older woman I met remembered that her grandparents had grown amaranth, but at the time she said it was considered a poor person's food, and had fallen out of favor. Many of the women we talked with at the time were somewhat familiar with a food product called alegria, which is made from amaranth, but the small amount of alegria brought into Oaxaca came from other parts of Mexico; at that time most Oaxacan people didn't know that the main ingredient in alegria is amaranth. They also had no idea what a field of amaranth even looked like. It was completely unfamiliar to them.

The reason we ended up traveling in a VW Bug from village to village was rooted in conversations Kate and I had the previous year after meeting in southern Mexico. In 2002 we were both involved with separate volunteer projects in that region. In my case, I had gone to Mexico because of my interest in addressing community health issues, particularly for pregnant mothers and children. At the time, there was particular concern about women's reproductive health, with one of the problems being spina bifida and other neural tube defects caused by a lack of folic acid in the diet. On my first trip to Mexico, I actually knew nothing about amaranth and was introduced to the crop by people like Kate who had been learning about it's potential for helping address some of the health issues that I and others were working on. The idea for a non-profit effort on community health first took root for us in 2002, and we decided to move to Oaxaca full-time in the spring of 2003 and see what we could do to help. Little did we know how much our work would become wrapped up with amaranth, or the directions that the work would take in setting Puente up as a non-profit.

We started with the simple and perhaps naive idea that if we could just get the rural families to use more amaranth in their diet that community health would be greatly improved. In 2000, government data indicated that 40% of rural children in Oaxaca were stunted in growth, just one of the serious health issues that was occurring from chronic malnutrition and an over-reliance on one primary food source, which was corn (maize). This led us in 2003 to work with health centers and health departments, trying to train doctors and other health workers to promote amaranth to villagers. Our particular focus was pregnant women and children under 5, many of whom were malnourished.

As time went on, it became apparent that the challenges we were facing were more complex than we first realized, and that it wasn't enough to just teach people how to cook with amaranth or give them some seed to grow a patch of it in their garden. We really needed more of a comprehensive or systems approach to the whole problem, which included getting access to appropriate grain amaranth varieties for planting, teaching people how to grow and harvest amaranth in small fields, working on methods of processing the amaranth, and continuing to work on how to best incorporate amaranth into the diet. We also worked on helping villagers, particularly women, learn how to make amaranth products they could sell in the village markets to make income.

In 2006, we hired our first agronomist (a crop and soil expert) to help farmers with the details on how to grow amaranth in fields. One thing we learned was that we needed to customize the information on how to grow amaranth for the many different growing conditions in the region, with some farmers growing in a desert-like environment and others growing the crop at higher elevations in the mountains. Although we initially focused on male farmers, we gradually realized we could generally make the most progress by working with women, some of whom grew the amaranth, others of whom came up with new products they could make and sell utilizing amaranth.

The aspect of our work of which I am most proud is that, over time, we managed to build community ownership in using

A Mexican teen in the state of Oaxaca with an armful of amaranth plants. Photo credit: Stan Cruz

Local community promoter transplanting amaranth in Oaxaca, Mexico. Photo credit: Roque Reyes

Children lining up to eat amaranth during Puente's annual summer nutrition camp.
Photo credit: Roque Reyes

amaranth and developing markets for it. One of our biggest shifts in thinking was not so much what we did, but how we went about our work. We found we really needed to get community members providing leadership and make sure the projects are very participatory. This type of approach, particularly in the last 5-6 years for Puente, has led to more lasting impact.

I heard time and time again from mothers who talked about a child being malnourished, and, after starting to feed the child amaranth on a regular basis, they saw a positive response, with the child gaining weight and doing better. I don't want to go overboard on any health claims, but instead want to encourage researchers and health workers to look more into the potential of amaranth to help with people who may be malnourished. We have seen some amazing results with amaranth that need more investigation.

One of my favorite success stories in the villages we have worked with is a rural woman telling me that she had done well enough selling amaranth products that her husband had quit his job and come to work for her! That's a real change in economic structure and is just one of many life-changing examples from villagers who have gotten involved with amaranth. While overall change in the region has been slow, by making a long-term effort with amaranth, we've seen clear progress. Going forward, more scaling up of amaranth production, processing, and products will be helpful to further boost rural economic opportunities and help more people have access to amaranth for their diet.

Overall, from 2003 to today, Puente has been able to deeply impact dozens of communities and has directly or indirectly contributed to more modest change in perhaps as many as 200 communities in southern Mexico. We are glad that we've been able to help so many indigenous farm families. Really the key part of our success has been the many local people who have contributed time and energy to the efforts to redevelop amaranth as a crop, food source, and economic driver for the region.

Building impacts through a community-based approach with amaranth
By Pete Noll [3]

I never could have imagined how one tiny seed would transform my life. The seed is, of course, amaranth, or in nahuatl, "huauht-li." If I had known at the time that its meaning was "the smallest giver of life," I might have been more prepared for the journey ahead. What follows is my personal and professional testimony with amaranth, primarily in Mexico, which began in 2008 when I started working at Puente a la Salud Comunitaria (Puente), in English "Bridges to Community Health," in Oaxaca, Mexico.

When I arrived at Puente, the organization had just launched an ambitious project to grow amaranth in four of the eight regions in Oaxaca. They had recently hired two young, hungry, and talented Mexican agronomists, Rigoberto Pola and Uriel Baeza. The leadership at Puente had identified an opportunity to fill an emergent need in the communities where we were promoting the consumption of amaranth. The opportunity was to help farmers grow grain and vegetable amaranth to give the families local access to this super food. For the past five years, the Puente team had primarily focused on working with young women to integrate amaranth into their diets to combat disproportionate rates of malnutrition in more than 60 communities in rural Oaxaca. But if there was no local production, the communities would have to depend on Puente to bring the amaranth in from long distances with the associated high costs. At that time, Puente only operated two very well-traveled VW Bugs!

Having identified that many of the participant women and their spouses worked in agriculture, Puente correctly seized on this opportunity to add a new project that would provide small-scale growers with amaranth seed, organic inputs, technical assistance and later, access to appropriate technology for harvesting, clean-

---

3 *Pete Noll is Executive Director of Puente a la Salud Comunitaria, and has worked at Puente in Oaxaca, Mexico, since 2009. Earlier in his career he worked with other non-profit organizations in Latin America and served in the Peace Corp in Guatamala.*

94

ing and popping grain amaranth. At Puente, I soon discovered that our work depended on an intervention that would not only find solutions for the plant, but also resonate with the people.

Puente would have to be a quick study to assure a seed that could adapt to the climate and soil conditions. Oaxaca is known for its bio-diversity and varying geographic and climatic conditions. The altitude ranges in our communities goes from 1,500 to 3,000 m above sea level, while rainfall can vary from 300 to 1,500 mm annually, depending on the location and year. Soil erosion is another critical factor. The agronomists would have to be able to provide timely accurate recommendations on when to sow the crop, the distance between plants, plant nutrition, and other crop management practices. Fortunately, we were able to tap into some pre-existing pioneers in amaranth in Mexico, primarily the nonprofit Centeotl, Alejandro Ortiz, Dr. Benito Manrique de Lara, and Dr. Eduardo Espitia.   In the later years, we would discover other expertise in Puebla, Morelos, Xochimilco, Queretaro and Tlaxcala.

In Oaxaca, Centeotl and Alejandro were early adopters and shared with us their experience in growing and transforming (or processing) amaranth into snack bars and pre-mix drinks. On

Jessica Vargas, a Puente agronomist in the Mixteca region, with a field of amaranth in the background. Photo credit: Roque Reyes

a national and international level, Dr. Manrique and Dr. Espitia were on the frontier of amaranth investigation, the latter having even studied at the Rodale Institute in Pennsylvania. Both Dr. Manrique and Dr. Espitia had participated with the Amaranth Institute, as part of the Mexican representation. Having such knowledgeable and committed allies allowed Puente to shorten significantly our learning curve with the agronomical aspects of growing amaranth. So, at an early stage, we now felt mostly confident that we had the technical "know-how" and, as Dr. Benito often reminded us, the "know-how not" and tools to properly (or ethically) approach the farming communities in the Mixe, Sierra Sur, Mixteca Alta and Central Valleys. So, in 2008, our technical team and promoters went off into the communities to offer to help them grow amaranth "plants" and thus diversify their farms.

But what could not be overlooked is how the "people" would take to our invitation. While amaranth was a significant part of the Mesoamerican culture as long as 6,000 years ago, it had become a mostly forgotten food. There are several versions, often debated, about why amaranth might have been almost eradicated from its peak production of 30,000 tons at the time of the Spanish conquest. But what we do know is that amaranth was mostly unknown to farmers in Oaxacan communities when Puente started in 2003. Add to the equation that Oaxaca is a unique context in that it is home to 40 to 50% of the indigenous-speaking population in all of Mexico, consisting of 16 spoken languages. Thus, there were many cultural and social aspects that we would have to better understand, to have any chance of gaining trust and credibility in the communities and with the farmers.

Like many other nonprofits, we decided to seek out local stakeholders and offer them training to develop them into amaranth community promoters. They spoke the local languages and had experience with local cropping systems, and thus were best able to facilitate the interaction between our technical staff and the growers. Even with a sound strategy in place, we relied on a lot of trial-and-error in the early years. As of 2018, we are now working with over 200 farmers and have incorporated more recently, using agro-ecological practices that include crop rotation, composting and other organic-based farm inputs.

In addition to the local promoters, we sought out ways to involve the local people's participation and empower them to make their own decisions about how to incorporate amaranth into their diets, farms and micro-enterprises. This holistic approach again meant investing both in the plant and the people, to assure we combined local wisdom, empirical and scientific knowledge. Today, we promote farmer-to-farmer (or campesino-a-campesino) exchanges, as this methodology has been a successful way to train directly and locally. Also, in 2013, Puente facilitated a process that led to the formation of two regional amaranth networks/cooperatives that are regionally run and managed by key community leaders. Our goal is that in the relatively near future, they will be fully self-managed and responsible for their collective actions.

In the Healthy Families program, Puente's flagship initiative, we have tried a lot of different strategies. Apart from a traditional snack made with amaranth, called la alegria (translated to joy), it is important to note again that amaranth was not in the local diet when Puente began promoting it for community health. The adoption or incorporation of a perceived new food is a challenge across the world. As we slowly had success in increasing the consumption of amaranth in the communities, we also learned a valuable lesson in 2014. As part of our volunteer program, we hosted a Spanish doctor and nutritionist for a two-month period. He noticed that in some of the cooking and nutrition workshops that we had women suffering from diabetes and other related diseases that stem from poor diets and eating habits. He recommended that we needed to substitute unhealthier options with amaranth, instead of just adding amaranth in the food preparation. Today, we have hundreds of recipes, developed in the communities or with our chef and gastronomy initiatives. We are making an intentional effort to ensure that the food that is prepared is nutritious and the added ingredients don't take away from amaranth's remarkable nutrition. The plant is versatile as you can eat the leaf and the grain. One popular recipe is to dice up the amaranth leaves when they are still tender and add them to lemon water.

In much the same way that we added the amaranth farming project in 2008, as Puente evolved and learned, we were in a position to address another important need in the communities. With the minimum wage at $5 per day, families were looking to diversify and increase their income streams. One obvious opportunity was to grow amaranth, a high value crop. However, since we work on small-scale production, often less than 250 pounds per harvest, the possibly greater opportunity lay in processing the amaranth into ready-to-eat products, especially popped amaranth.

Here is where our collaboration with Dr. Benito Manrique and his organization, San Miguel de Proyectos Agropecuarios, bore enormous fruits for Puente. He had been innovating a micro-popping machine that could be used at the community level. Much like Oaxacan families take their corn to the mill to be made into tortilla dough, the mini-popper could provide a similar function. (Include a photo). The mini-popper essentially allowed the farmers to double the value of their amaranth with minimal cost and effort. A pound of unpopped amaranth could be sold for $.75 per pound while popped amaranth was $1.50 or more per pound. Since Dr. Manrique's ultimate vision was to offer amaranth to the most marginalized communities, he was ecstatic to have Puente invite the local farming cooperatives to try out the machine and expand the consumption of amaranth in Oaxaca. To this day, the mini-poppers continue to pop out 20 pounds of amaranth per hour that is purchased by the micro-enterprise groups and general consumers in Oaxaca, primarily. And this is where our newest program, Social Economy, took life.

Due to this increased demand for amaranth and the need for families to generate additional income, we began to help family start-

Left photo. Amaranth grain being popped with technology developed by San Miguel de Proyectos Agropecuarios, SPR. Photo credit: Nikhol Esteras Roberts

Top photo. Amaranth balls, known as "Tzoallis," made of toasted corn, agave and popped amaranth. Photo credit: Roque Reyes

ups, mostly women, form micro-enterprises. Seven years later, we have 25 micro-enterprise groups that sell amaranth products and generate much-needed income for their families and communities. In many ways, our approach is like the US concept of Farm-to-Table, as we encourage the farmers to keep part of their harvest for local consumption. While this approach might seem obvious, the reality in Mexico was the opposite. We have spoken with many farmers in Puebla who have been growing amaranth for up to 25 years, and yet have never eaten it.

But growing, consuming and selling amaranth isn't the whole story. I want to share one personal and fascinating learning experience. Upon my arrival, I noticed that Puente had an activity that aimed to throw a party to celebrate the harvest. My initial reaction was that with limited resources, would throwing a party be the best utilization of our budget? How wrong I was, as the celebrations have morphed into a Puente-hosted, state-wide amaranth food fair with more than 10,000 people attending every October to commemorate World Food Day. I will never forget the lesson I learned about the importance of respecting local customs and ideas.

Popped amaranth being sold in jars at an Oaxacan market as part of a Puente project. The jar slogan is translated into "I love amaranth!"
Photo credit: Roque Reyes

Field of amaranth in Oaxaca showing diversity of plant types.
Photo credit: Roque Reyes

Finally, it should be mentioned that Puente also includes attention to youth in our strategy, as the average age of the farmers in Mexico, like the U.S., is 60 years old. What will happen if Mexico skips a generation of farmers? Somewhat related, Puente has targeted work in public policy to promote investment in sustainable agriculture, offering healthy alternatives, with amaranth in school breakfast programs, and we participate in a nation-wide initiative for a healthy, just and sustainable food system. There is no doubt that amaranth is an incredible food option, but we recognize the systematic nature of our work and thus, we continue to adjust our strategies, as needed.

This year, 2018, Puente celebrates our 15-year anniversary as a nonprofit, promoting and working with amaranth, the plant, and the people in Oaxaca. I have thoroughly enjoyed having the opportunity to share with you my perspective about how one seed influenced my past ten years. In my presentation, at the Amaranth Day in 2017, I titled my talk, "Amaranth, a small revolutionary," with the explanation that my concept of being a revolutionary was to bring about positive and lasting change. It is so exciting to dream about where amaranth will be in 15 years, not only in Oaxaca, but also across the continents.

CHAPTER 9

PLANTING AMARANTH

Growing amaranth is not unlike growing other vigorous summer crops like corn or beans. There are, however, some differences, including at the planting stage. This chapter will describe three approaches to planting amaranth:

- In a home garden
- On a small-scale farm with walk-behind push planters
- On a larger-scale farm with mechanical planters

Fortunately, all three approaches are fairly straightforward. Amaranth is a relatively easy crop to grow and, once it gets established, grows quickly.

General tips on planting: date, depth, rate, and row widths

For planting date, a rule of thumb with amaranth is to plant when the soil is at least 70 °F. (21 C.) In Missouri, where I live, that could happen in early May in a warm spring, but I generally wait until late May or even early June to plant grain amaranth. There are some advantages to waiting to plant, especially if you are growing a legume cover crop to provide nitrogen and need to give it extra time to grow before terminating the legume. A later planting date may help with weed control, especially if tillage is involved, as it gives early season weeds time to sprout and then they can be killed by pre-plant tillage or other methods.

The latest time window I have been able to successfully plant amaranth in central Missouri is early July, assuming the goal is to fall-harvest seed. Vegetable types could be planted later, since they don't need to grow as long before leaf harvest.

Keep in mind that amaranth has very small round seeds (about 1 mm or 0.04 inch in diameter) and they need to be planted shallow, not more than 1/2 inch deep (or roughly a cm) in most soils. The tiny seeds don't have enough stored energy, unlike bigger seeds, to come up if planted very deep in the soil. They are also sensitive to soil crusting, since the tiny seedlings don't have a lot of strength to push through crusted soil that may form after a heavy rain.

When planting amaranth in a large field with a field crop planter, I usually plant about 2 pounds per acre (2.2 kg per hectare). When planting by hand in my garden or small demonstration sites, I've found that I don't need to be too particular about seeding rate and can just quickly walk along and sprinkle in some seeds. This is because of amaranth's ability to self-thin, as described in more detail in the next section under "Planting amaranth in your garden."

Row width is more important for amaranth than seeding rate. I did two years of field research experimenting with different row widths for three different varieties of grain amaranth. They all performed best at 30 inch row spacing (0.76 m), and worst at 7.5 inch row spacing. I also tried a 15 inch row spacing, and while that was somewhat better than the narrowest rows, it was significantly worse than the wider 30 inch rows. My observation is that the amaranth plants start to compete with each other too much in the narrower row settings, leading to shorter plants and smaller seed heads, with lower yields. I even noticed the narrow row spacing having a lighter green color as if they were more stressed. Because of this, stick to rows of about 30 to 36 inches whether planting by machine or hand. I don't recommend rows wider than this, however, because the leaves may not shade out the inter-row area if the rows are farther than about 36 inches apart. That shading is important for weed control.

Planting amaranth in your garden

If you are a home gardener who is familiar with growing direct seeded crops planted in a row, you can easily grow amaranth. As with other summer crops, it's probably simplest to plant into recently tilled soil, taking a hoe and making a long shallow trench. You will want to keep the furrows you make very shallow. If the soil is loose enough, try to cover the amaranth seeds with at least 1/8 inch of soil, but not more than 1/2 inch (1.27 cm).

If planting a small area, I like to make small ridges, 4 to 6 inches (10-15 cm) high, in which to plant amaranth and other summer garden plants. On my heavy clay soils, it helps with drainage, especially if it rains a lot. If you have lighter textured soils (sandier or loamy), you won't need to worry about making a ridge. Also, when planting a large area, I probably wouldn't take time to make ridges.

The good news with hand planting amaranth seeds is that you can do it quickly and don't need to be precise with how much you're planting. That's because of amaranth's interesting ability to self-thin, which means that any extra seedlings that emerge tend to die off or not grow much. Whether you plant 1000 seeds every foot of row or 10 seeds every foot (30 cm), my experience has been that you still end up with about 1-4 mature plants per foot of row. In other words, with 1000 seeds planted in a foot of row, only one may turn into a full-sized plant, though you'll see dozens or hundreds of seedlings initially emerge in that foot of row. Most of those tiny seedlings just stop growing and disappear; a few will grow into small plants, generally topping out at a few inches to a foot tall.

The reason for this remarkable self-thinning with amaranth has to do in part with the "plasticity" of the plant's growth. The seedlings that get off to the fastest start outcompete their neighbors and keep growing fast, while the neighboring plants seem to either die or grow very slowly. This is quite different from a crop like corn, where overcrowding the seeds in a row of plants will usually lead to all the corn plants being small.

Due to amaranth's self-thinning nature, there is no need to worry about an exact seeding rate. When planting in the garden I prefer to err on the high side and sprinkle plenty of seeds into the row. Unlike carrots, potatoes, or other space-sensitive plants, you never need to worry about thinning out the stand of amaranth by hand, because it will self-thin. Sprinkle the seeds liberally, moving along at a good pace, then cover them with a shallow layer of soil. I normally plant a hundred seeds or more per foot of row, but I really don't worry about the particular amount of seed, which is part of what makes planting amaranth easy! I can generally plant 50 row feet (15 m) of amaranth by hand-seeding in just 5-10 minutes, including making the furrow and covering the seeds up with a hoe. After I cover the seed with soil, I go back along and tamp down or firm the soil in the seed row with the back of the hoe or by lightly pressing my foot on the row. If the soil is moist with high clay content, be careful not to over-compact it, or the seeds may have trouble emerging.

In regard to watering the newly planted seeds, my advice depends on your soil type. If you have a sandy or loamy soil, by all means go ahead and water the newly planted seeds right after planting and again every couple of days until they are well-established, assuming it's not raining. On the other hand, if you have a heavy clay loam soil like me, you need to be more careful about watering. I've had experiences where I watered the newly planted seed rows because no rain was forecast and the soil was dry, then went out of town on a work trip, only to come home several days later and find that few plants had emerged due to crusting of the soil. Thus, I've learned to err on the side of leaving the seeds unwatered unless I think I can be attentive to keeping the soil moist for a few days until the seeds emerged.

Amaranth has a remarkable ability to sprout in seemingly dry soils that would have left other seeds, such as beans and corn, sitting there unsprouted. I attribute this at least in part to the tiny size of amaranth seeds, which allows them to get good seed-to-soil contact and probably helps with moisture uptake. As I'll note later in the section on machine planting, I've learned over the years that it is better to plant amaranth when there's no rain in the forecast, at least in heavy soils, to avoid issues with crusting. Even though the soil might seem dry, as long as it's not too cloddy and the seed row is firmed up by hand or machine, the seed will often emerge. Of course there are limits – not even amaranth will come up in a bone dry soil!

I have grown amaranth in my garden for about 25 years, and most times I plant it into tilled soil. However, I have experimented with "no-till" planting of amaranth in my garden, as well as in farm fields. No-till planting of amaranth by hand in a garden is actually not too hard, but you have to think about managing insects when there is extra residue (leaves and stems) on the plant surface that gives them a place to hide. Many insects love chomping on amaranth seedlings, and while insects aren't usually a problem for amaranth seedlings in a tilled garden, they can be problematic in a no-till situation. You can reduce the chance of this problem by using a hoe to create a small cleared strip at least a few inches wide before making your shallow furrow for the amaranth seeds. You also need to time your no-till planting so that the soil is moderately but not excessively moist, allowing you to scrape some loose soil back over the seeds.

A labor-intensive option for hand planting is the use of transplants. The only situation where I can envision a home gardener bothering with amaranth transplants is if you are just growing a few as ornamental flowering plants in a flower bed where you want to control the spacing of everything you are planting.

Planting amaranth on a small-scale farm with walk-behind push planters

If you are planting no more than few thousand square feet of amaranth, it will be manageable to plant by hand. However, if you want to plant a quarter acre or even up to an acre, I'd recommend using a push planter. You'll be able to cover considerably more ground with much less bending over. There are a few walk-behind push planter models on the market from companies such as Earthways, Glaser, and Jang. They start at a little over $100 and go up to $400-500 depending on the model you buy. You will need to experiment on which seed plate to use, but because amaranth is not very sensitive to seeding rate, probably a few different seed plates or "wheels" can be used.

As with hand planting, you'll need to decide whether to till the soil before planting amaranth or try no-till planting. Push planters are designed to work best in somewhat loose tilled soil, but if the soil conditions are right (a little moisture but not too wet, and not too much residue), you may be able to use one in a no-till situation. I'd suggest experimenting with a few different approaches to see what works best for you, rather than going out and planting a whole acre with only one approach that might not work very well.

Planting amaranth on a larger scale with mechanical equipment

I've had the opportunity to use several different field crop planters in growing amaranth. Almost anything used to plant corn, soybeans, wheat, or other grains can be used with amaranth, although some minor modification may be needed. The one type of planter set up I would avoid using is an air seeder, where the planter has a large "drum" designed with hundreds of holes for large seeds like corn or beans; that would definitely not work with tiny amaranth seeds!

Fortunately, most grain drills and row crop planters will work fine. With drills, I've found that amaranth does not respond well to planting in narrow rows. The crop will initially grow fine, but once the plants are big enough to compete between the narrow rows, they start to crowd each other too much, as noted earlier in this chapter. Thus, to use a grain drill, I recommend closing off some of the rows with tape so that an effective row width of around 30 inches (0.76 m) is achieved. The other challenge with a drill is to keep the flow rate of the seed low enough. You only need about 1 to 2 pounds of amaranth planted per acre (roughly 1 to 2 kg per hectare). This can be tough to achieve on a drill designed to plant much higher rates of seed. A drill equipped with a "small seed" box will generally work better at achieving a low seeding rate, but it just depends on drill design.

The best way I have found to mechanically plant amaranth is to use the insecticide boxes that typically come with basic row crop planters. The insecticide boxes are designed to meter out very low amounts of granular insecticide, which is similar to distributing a pound or two per acre of tiny amaranth seed. Although you can't necessarily use the same insecticide box setting as the manual may recommend for two pounds of insecticide, with a little trial and error you can find a setting that will allow an appropriate flow of amaranth seed (the amaranth flows out of the box at a little different rate than most granular insecticides).

The one modification I usually make when planting with insecticide boxes on a row crop planter is to buy some bulk length Tygon® tubing so that I can install a longer length than what the insecticide box comes standard with. Normally, the goal with the insecticide application is to scatter the insecticide granules over the ground near the seed row, but not necessarily in the furrow. However, with the amaranth seed, you want it to go in the furrow, so you need a longer length of tube to crop it more directly into the furrow. This tubing is available at almost any equipment dealer selling planters and is very inexpensive. Modifying a 4-row planter should cost less than $30-40 in new tubing and take only a few minutes per row to install. Another advantage of using new tubing besides just the longer length is that it facilitates good seed flow, compared to an old tube that may be full of spider webs and debris that can trap the seed.

Occasionally I've needed to use some baling wire to get the end of the plastic tube from the insecticide box right over the furrow where I want it, but usually there's a good place to feed it down through the brackets holding the furrow openers. I don't get too concerned if part of the seed ends up on top of the furrow. In fact, one of the things I like about this method of seeding is that you usually end up with seed at a variety of depths. Most should be at the bottom of the furrow, but some will end up at shallower depths because of the way the closing wheels push the soil back into the furrow just as the amaranth seed is falling in there. With the large number of seeds at various depths, it increased the odds that some of the seeds will be at the right depth.

Again, it's a different way of thinking about seeding rate than with corn or soybean seeds, when you want every seed to grow to maturity. With amaranth, if you are seeding 2 pounds an acre, that's a million seeds per acre. Even if most of those seeds emerge, by the time of harvest, it's normal to have only about 20,000-40,000 full-sized plants, so you really only need about one out of every 50 seeds to emerge, assuming they do so evenly.

I typically try to plant about 2 pounds of amaranth seed per acre with the insecticide box system. I've done replicated field trials with various amaranth varieties at seeding rates of 0.25, 0.5, 1.0, 2.0, and 4.0 pounds of seed per acre (1 pound per acre = 1.12 kilograms per hectare). There were no significant differences in yield among any of those seeding rates, which is remarkable. I know of no other field crop that you can vary the seeding rate by 16-fold without having a yield impact!

To make sure you are getting good seed flow, I like to have one person walk behind the planter for a minute or two when starting out and watch to see if the seed is flowing well. The seed can be a little hard to see in the soil, so watching it flow into the furrow is helpful. This is easier if it's a sunny day and the light reflects off the flowing seeds. Seed monitors normally won't be of help when using the insecticide boxes, so a second set of eyes is valuable. If you don't have a helper around, try driving the planter a few feet over concrete, a tarp, or even some pieces of cardboard to see if the seed is coming out well.

As mentioned earlier in this chapter, amaranth seeds are not particularly vigorous in the sense of being able to force their way up through heavy soil or especially a crusted soil, so shallow seeding is a must. I try to plant about 1/2 inch deep (1.27 cm) with a planter, but a shallower depth can work. In a light-textured sandy soil it might be possible to plant the amaranth a little deeper, but I haven't grown amaranth in that soil type.

In preparing ground to plant amaranth, I have normally prepared a "fine" seedbed with tillage equipment, trying to avoid a rough cloddy field (see more details in the previous chapter on "managing the soil"). I have no-till planted amaranth a few times with planters, and it is more challenging than planting in tilled soil, but can be done. The main challenge is placing the amaranth at a shallow enough depth in no-till. Attention also needs to be paid to insects that may hide in no-till residue and attack the emerging seedlings.

Overall, following the tips above, you should be able to have success planting amaranth. It requires a little more care and attention than planting crops with more vigorous seedlings like corn and beans, but the high number of amaranth seeds typically planted and their ability to self-thin compensates somewhat for the modest vigor of the seedlings.

One other thing to be aware of when planting amaranth is that it has a tendency to emerge quickly but then not grow very much for a week or so while the roots are getting going. Then it will start to take off and grow quickly. So don't be alarmed if the seedlings don't seem to be doing much during the first days after they emerge – the action is below ground first, and once the roots have tapped into some nutrients, then the above ground growth will kick into gear.

Photo of an amaranth planting date research study by the author in central Missouri, comparing multiple varieties of grain amaranth.

CHAPTER 10

MANAGING SOIL PREPARATION AND SOIL FERTILITY FOR AMARANTH

As with any crop, successful production of amaranth involves having a good plan for plant nutrition and having a seedbed appropriate to amaranth growing needs. This is true whether you are growing a small garden plot or a large field. Fortunately, amaranth will grow in a range of soil types, from heavy clay soils to lighter-textured sandy loam soils. Soil pH should ideally be in a range of about 6.0 to 8.0, but amaranth can tolerate as low as about 5.5 pH.

In my experience, amaranth needs only a moderate amount of nitrogen fertility: not nearly as much as corn but comparable to plants such as sunflowers. I did a replicated field research project years ago to look at rates of nitrogen fertilization on various amaranth varieties. Test levels were 0, 40, 80, 120, and 160 pounds of nitrogen per acre. Optimum yields were generally obtained at 80 pounds of nitrogen per acre, and higher rates provided no significant benefit.

Phosphorous (P) and potassium (K) fertilizer may not be needed in a typical garden setting, depending on whether compost is used and the organic matter level of the soil. In a commercial field, I would use a soil test to determine if P and K are needed. The test lab won't have a standard recommendation for amaranth, so ask the lab to provide a recommendation for soybeans or sorghum and use that to guide you on amount of P and K to consider applying. Little is known about whether amaranth has any particular micronutrient needs. I think on a reasonably productive soil, it is unlikely to need any special micronutrient application. For a garden, a little compost is always a good thing for soil improvement, but application of compost is not usually practical on a large field scale.

Use of cover crops with amaranth

Since amaranth needs only a modest amount of nitrogen, I have found that use of a legume cover crop can supply sufficient nitrogen, provided that the legume is allowed to grow for long enough. In Missouri, I personally prefer crimson clover before amaranth, but I have also used hairy vetch with success. I find crimson clover to be easier to terminate (kill) and easier to till with a rototiller, as well as easier to directly seed into for no-till planting compared to hairy vetch. Additionally, crimson clover tends to get a bit more fall growth than hairy vetch. Austrian winter peas are another viable legume to use before amaranth, and there are other clovers that may work in certain situations, such as balansa clover, yellow sweet clover, and berseem clover, or in more northern areas, red clover can be used.

When growing crimson clover in Missouri, I generally try to plant it by the end of September if possible, but have had success planting it in mid-October; just be aware that the later it is planted, the less likely winter survival will be. Crimson clover is better suited for the southern half of the U.S. (such as south of Interstate 70, as a rough delineation) because it often won't overwinter in more northern areas. I recommend red clover for more northern growing areas, but some testing of balansa clover may be worthwhile.

If I'm using crimson clover in the garden, I broadcast it by hand or with a seed/fertilizer spinner spreader. I sometimes broadcast the seed while I still have vegetables growing in the garden. The clover won't hurt any garden plants still growing in the fall. If I can lightly rake in the clover seed (or other cover crop seed), I will do that to improve seed-to-soil contact; otherwise I try to time the cover crop seeding before a rain or use a sprinkler periodically for a few days to encourage growth.

My approach to terminating crimson clover and other legumes before planting amaranth or other crops depends on whether I am in a garden or large field setting. If in a small garden, I normally run a rototiller through the clover. If the clover or other legume is tall, I sometimes run a push mower or string trimmer (weed whacker) through it first to reduce the amount of cover crop stems wrapping around the tiller tines. This is especially true if using hairy vetch – the vines of vetch can tangle a tiller up in a hurry!

If I want to no-till plant in a garden while using a cover, then I definitely mow it, waiting until the cover crop has flowered. There are small-scale roller-crimper machines available that I have seen used to terminate a cover crop, but I haven't tried the walk-behind type, just the tractor-mounted ones. After mowing the cover crop, I will use a hoe to prepare or furrow. If there is a lot of biomass, it may be necessary to rake some of the biomass aside from the planting zone. I've also tried taking compost and creating a planting strip a few inches wide and an inch or so deep with compost. I've had mixed success with that – it saves having to rake aside the cover crop residue, but you have to work to keep the compost moist or the seeds may dry out.

In the short term, tilling the cover crop in with a rototiller (if you have one), is probably the easiest way to get a good stand of am-aranth in the garden. However, research shows that soil health is improved by minimizing soil disturbance. The tilling action of the rototiller tears up macropores created by earthworms and cover crop roots, and also damages fungi in the soil that might otherwise help with crop growth, particularly mycorrhizal fungi. Therefore, the less tilling you do, the better.

If a commercial field setting, I recommend using a grain drill to plant clover or other cover crop seed. If no drill is available, the seed can be broadcast and then lightly tilled in with a harrow, vertical tillage tool, or other shallow tillage device. Or, if the soil surface is bare, it may be possible to just broadcast the seed before a rain and not do any tillage. To terminate crimson clover or other legumes in a large field, strong planning is necessary.

For organic operations, I'd either till in the clover, or if no-till is desired, wait until it has flowered and then either mow it as close to the ground as possible or use a roller-crimper on it. Use of a roller-crimper is more likely to completely kill the clover than a mower, but if using a roller-crimper, avoid doing it when the ground is wet. A second pass of the roller-crimper may be needed if a thick mat of cover crop plants is present.

For conventional operations (non-organic), herbicides can be used to terminate the clover or other cover crops. Many cover crops are killed effectively by glyphosate alone, but clover and other legumes are difficult to kill with just glyphosate, so it's best to add 2,4-D to the tank mix.

To get optimum nitrogen contribution from crimson clover or other legumes, I'd suggest waiting to terminate them until they have flowered. That timing varies for different legume species. In Missouri, I normally terminate the cover crops crimson clover or hairy vetch in late May (after the cover crop has flowered) and then plant the amaranth soon after, often the same day.

Do not use cereal rye before amaranth

Cereal rye is a great cover crop to use before many cash crops, particularly soybeans and other bean crops. However, in the two years I spent working with a graduate student to test using it before amaranth, it appeared to have negative allelopathic effects on the amaranth: the amaranth planted after rye cover crop was smaller, lighter green in color, and much lower yielding than amaranth planted after legumes or where there was no cover crop used. Supplemental nitrogen fertilizer partially offset the effects of rye but not completely. It appeared the impact of the rye went beyond just limiting the nitrogen available to the amaranth to a negative allelopathic impact. Additionally, rye is known to have an ability to suppress small-seeded broadleaf weeds, such as the pigweed cousins of amaranth.

If a cereal cover crop is to be used before amaranth, either alone or in a cover crop mix, I'd recommend oats or wheat as much safer choices to use than cereal rye or even triticale (triticale is a

Amaranth on the left was following cereal rye, and growth was severely impacted. The first four rows to the right of the shortest plants received a high rate of nitrogen fertilizer which partially compensated for the negative impact of the rye, but yields were still substantially depressed compared to amaranth on the far right of the photo that was grown where there was no rye.

cross of wheat and rye)

Preparing the soil for planting

As a small-seeded crop, amaranth needs either a finely-tilled field (no big clods) or a no-till planting approach where good seed-to-soil contact can be obtained. Farmers growing amaranth organically have typically done a few tillage passes to get the field ready and prepare a crumbly seed-bed. With a roller-crimper and a good no-till planter, it's possible to grow no-till amaranth organically, but ONLY if a good biomass mat of cover crops is obtained to smother the weeds. That would normally be easiest by growing cereal rye as a cover, but as noted above, this is not recommended for amaranth; this makes it tough to grow amaranth organically *and* do no-till. Doing just one of these two management approaches (organic or no-till) is more viable.

Since there are no labeled herbicides for amaranth, I've often used a "stale seed bed" technique. This involves doing one or more tillage passes in the spring to both prepare the seedbed and get weed seeds to sprout. Then, rather than planting right away after tillage, I wait 10-14 days while weeds start to grow. The day before planting amaranth, I spray glyphosate over the ground to kill the existing weeds, then I plant the amaranth without any further tillage. By not tilling at the time of planting amaranth, I reduce the number of new weed seedlings following the herbicide spray. This way, the amaranth can get off to a good weed-free start and usually gets a few weeks' head start on other weeds that may emerge. However, you can expect more weeds will eventually emerge, so some mechanical or hand weeding will be needed later in the season.

One other tip on early season field operations is to avoid using a rotary hoe. Organic farmers often use a rotary hoe after crops like corn and soybeans emerge to disrupt weeds right when they emerge. The rotary hoe tines will flick out small weeds that have sprouted at the soil surface, but not the more deeply rooted and anchored corn or soybean plants. However, amaranth starts out shallow and grows slowly at first, meaning that the rotary hoe is as likely to kill the amaranth plants as it is to kill the weeds. Therefore, I've avoided rotary hoeing. Instead, using a row crop cultivator after amaranth is 12 to 24 inches tall (0.3 to 0.6 m) is often helpful for weed control, so I recommend having a row crop cultivator available if possible when farming with tillage.

CHAPTER 11
MANAGING WEEDS AND PESTS IN AMARANTH PRODUCTION

Weeds are a challenge in growing any crop, including amaranth. Diseases and insects can also reduce seed yield and quality of an otherwise promising harvest. Fortunately, amaranth is a relatively vigorous crop that, once established, competes well with weeds, and is generally free of serious disease issues. A number of insect pests are attracted to amaranth, as described in more detail below, but most do only minor damage to the crop. This chapter will describe managing pests in both gardens and commercial fields, and outline organic and conventional methods of dealing with potential pest problems.

Managing weeds in amaranth

Early-season weed control is particularly important with amaranth due to its slow growth during the first couple of weeks after emergence. If weeds get an early jump on the amaranth, it will greatly curtail growth of the amaranth plants. Once the amaranth is a few feet tall and has enough leaves to shade out the areas between rows, weed control becomes a lesser concern. As a crop that will reach 5-7 feet in height, depending on variety, rainfall, and soil quality, it can outgrow many shorter weeds. However, care should be given to eliminating other members of the pigweed family that may appear as weeds in an amaranth field, especially if some of the seed is going to be kept for the next growing season. While most of the cousins of grain amaranth among the *Amaranthus* (pigweed) genus will not hybridize with grain amaranth, at least a couple of species have the potential to hybridize. Usually the offspring of a weedy pigweed and grain amaranth either produces no seed or produces seed that will not germinate, but it's best to avoid creating those weedy hybrids in your seed supply by keeping the various types of pigweeds out of your grain amaranth.

In the garden

The most important time to control weeds in your garden is right after your plantings start growing, whether they are amaranth or another crop. You either need to have a mulch in place right away (from a cover crop or by spreading straw, grass clippings, or newspaper) or get out a hoe and start weeding. I've gone the route of using a cover crop mulch (it works pretty well if you have a thick even stand of cover crop), or adding a mulch (I've done both straw and grass clippings, depending on the year), and I've also just relied on early hoeing with no mulch some years.

In a small garden, hoeing weeds doesn't have to take long. I often go out and hoe for 5-10 minutes in the cool of the morning before I go to my office, and do that for the first few weeks of the growing season. After that, I may only need to hoe once a week in the middle of the summer, and not at all in late summer. I particularly like using a "collinear hoe," such as is sold by Johnny's Selected Seeds, because it has a long handle that involves less bending and the sharp narrow blade can very quickly scrape off small emerging weed seedlings without having to do much soil disturbance or a lot of chopping. The narrow blade also fits more easily between small amaranth plants (or other garden plants) more easily than a regular hoe if I need to swipe out a weed that is right in the row with the amaranth.

If you apply a mulch of grass clippings, be aware the grass clippings can tie up some nitrogen as they decompose. When I use grass clippings, I generally wait until the amaranth has gotten off to a good start and then apply a little nitrogen fertilizer before laying any grass clippings down between the rows. Straw can also require some supplemental nitrogen, but typically less than needed with grass clippings. Using a legume cover crop can take care of the nitrogen need, so in more recent years I've generally taken that approach with amaranth in my garden, using crimson clover or a mix of crimson clover and hairy vetch.

Weed management in commercial fields

If you are going to try growing amaranth in a multi-acre field, I suggest giving some serious thought to how you will control weeds, whether an organic or conventional approach will be used. If you want to take the organic approach, most likely you are going to be doing a fair bit of tillage for weed control. Below are three distinct approaches to weed control in grain amaranth fields.

Approach #1. Organic weed management using tillage.
Most people who have grown amaranth in organic fields have ended up using several tillage passes, typically 2-3 before planting and at least two cultivations with a tractor-mounted cultivator after the amaranth emerges. The pre-plant tillage is to help not only with seedbed preparation, as described in other chapters, but also to help with early season weed control. If a number of weeds are coming up at the time the amaranth is to be planted, they need to be killed before planting the amaranth, so some light tillage with a field cultivator or disk will likely be needed. I've also used tractor-mounted rototillers. Those prepare a nice seedbed for planting, but the downside is that they over-till the soil and tend to trigger a lot of weed seeds to sprout.

After the amaranth plants emerge, when growing amaranth organically I try to use at least two passes with a row crop cultivator, once when the amaranth is 6-12 inches tall and again when it's 20-30 inches tall. Once the amaranth gets to the height of the cultivator tool bar, you won't be able to drive through it any more that season. Sometimes I've used shields on the cultivator for the first cultivation pass of the season, to avoid burying or knocking over the young amaranth plants. After they get a foot tall or so, the shields will typically be taken off for subsequent cultivator passes.

Approach #2. Organic no-till weed management.
Growing amaranth organically in a no-till system is a challenging

proposition. First of all, while cereal rye is the best cover crop for no-till organic grain production in soybeans, I don't recommend it for use with amaranth due to allelopathic chemicals from the rye that inhibit growth of the amaranth. An alternative to rye is winter wheat, which doesn't have the allelochemicals. However, if wheat alone is grown before amaranth, the amaranth will end up being nitrogen-deficient in an organic system.

My suggestion would be to use a legume and oat cover crop mix and seed it thickly, using either crimson clover and/or hairy vetch with the oats. If using a legume alone, the high nitrogen residue of the legume will decompose too quickly and not provide much duration of weed control. Having oats in the mix will lengthen by at least a couple of weeks, possibly longer, the weed suppression from the cover crop. You'd need to use a roller crimper to terminate the cover crop either right before or shortly after planting. I'd suggest using the roller crimper after planting amaranth, as it's easier to plant before that thick mat of material is flattened to the ground.

I have two main cautions with this possible no-till organic system. The first is that it will be difficult to plant the amaranth at an appropriate shallow depth (1/2 inch or about 1.2 cm) in such a system, and the second is that late-season weed control may be challenging. I do believe this organic no-till system, if used with a good thick stand of cover crops, can work for early season weed control. In theory, a high residue (no-till) cultivator could be used for a single pass when the amaranth is a couple feet tall to take care of late emerging weeds, but then it would no longer be a true no-till system.

Approach #3. Conventional weed management.
There are no labeled post-emerge sprays or residual herbicide sprays for use with grain amaranth. In research plots, grass control herbicides like Poast and Select have been tolerated by amaranth for post-emerge control of weeds like foxtail, but unfortunately these products are not labeled for amaranth use.

However, burn-down herbicides such as Roundup (glyphosate) or Gramoxone (paraquat) can be used, provided it is before the amaranth is planted.

A technique I have found to work well is to lightly till the field to be planted to amaranth once or twice in early and/or mid-May. The goal of the tillage is to sprout as many weed seeds as possible. I then spray those weeds with glyphosate a day before I plant the amaranth seed. The amaranth planting is done without any further tilling in the stale seedbed planting technique as mentioned above under the first organic approach. This approach usually allows the amaranth to get off to a relatively weed-free start. This technique was also mentioned in the soil prep chapter.

To be sure, some other weeds will emerge as the season goes along. If you just have a few acres and the weed numbers are small, you can just hand weed them. However, on bigger or weedier fields, you'll need to have a row crop cultivator available and plan to drive the cultivator through the field at least once, if not twice. If doing it twice, I'd try to do the cultivation when the amaranth is about 6-12 inches tall and then again when it's about 20-30 inches tall. After that point, you have to hope the amaranth will shade out most of the late emerging weeds, because the amaranth will be too big to use a cultivator on later in the season.

The only other conventional herbicide tool that can legally be used on grain amaranth is a "rope-wick" type tool bar mounted on a tractor. Normally, this device is used with glyphosate, and the wick causes herbicide to be brushed onto any weeds that are taller than the amaranth at the time of application. Unfortunately, the rope-wick applicator helps not at all with any weeds shorter than the amaranth. Because of this, I generally prefer using a row crop cultivator that can kill a variety of weed sizes.

Managing insects in amaranth

Having grown amaranth for 24 years in Missouri and three summers in Maryland, my experience is that there are a lot of insects that like amaranth. Maybe this reflects that both the seed and leaves are good to eat? Fortunately, most of the many different insects I've seen eating or hanging out on amaranth do little damage. The time of greatest risk for the amaranth is when it first emerges. There have been a couple of times I lost most of my amaranth seedlings because insects came along and ate the tiny seedlings, usually at night. Although a broad spectrum granular insecticide could be used to kill insects that might attack seedlings, I personally would suggest not worrying about it and just replanting if you have a problem. The slight exception would be if you are planting amaranth into high residue where insect pressure is likely to be greater; in that situation you should be scouting daily as the amaranth emerges, but I would only apply an insecticide if really needed at the seedling stage.

Once the amaranth gets to be a few inches tall, the number of serious insect threats shrinks dramatically. The most consistent insect pest of consequence I've seen on amaranth is tarnished plant bug (*Lygus lineolaris*), which has shown up every year I've grown it, though it is worse some years than others. This insect, which is a small sucking insect about the size of a small ladybug, does little damage to amaranth until the seed starts to develop. Then it will move into the seed head and start sucking on individual seeds and sometimes the vascular tissues that feed parts of the flower head. Occasionally, a lygus bug will kill a whole section of an inflorescence (seed head) by disrupting the vascular tissues feeding that section of the seed head. More often, they damage the individual seeds in significant numbers, sucking the insides out of the seed and leaving a shriveled shell of the seed (see photo below). This pest can be controlled to some extent with broad spectrum insecticides like Sevin or organic products like pyrethrin, but I don't usually bother spraying for it. I would suggest keeping an eye on their numbers, and if they seem particularly thick (dozens per seed head), you may need to consider spraying an organic or synthetic product.

Photo above on left shows a portion of an amaranth inflorescence damaged by lygus bugs that have disrupted the vascular tissue in the grain head. Photo above on right shows individual seed damage caused by lygus bugs piercing the seed and sucking on contents. Photo below shows closeup of mature lygus bug.

Other insect pests that have occasionally caused serious damage in my fields are alfalfa webworms and blister beetles. I've seen webworm damage around the time flowers start to appear per-haps one year out of five, but only once in 27 years have I felt a need to spray for it; that year it was affecting nearly every plant in a small research field. The webworms can keep the amaranth inflorescence from developing normally, greatly reducing yield. Blister beetles are another infrequent pest, but colonies of blister beetles can completely defoliate plants, usually just in small patches of less than 50 square feet. Generally, they do their damage over a few day period, before moving onto a different part of the field. The spotty nature of their attacks makes it inefficient to treat a whole field for them.

Almost every year, I notice grasshoppers, various caterpillars, and other leaf feeding insects working away on the amaranth leaves. They can occasionally make the leaves look a bit ragged, but I haven't had a situation where I felt they were doing any real damage to the yield potential of the plant.

In short, scouting amaranth weekly for insect pests is not a bad idea, but insecticide applications are seldom needed, with the possible exception of sometimes needing to control lygus bugs. There are are a few organic products that can be used, including Bt for soft-bodied insects like caterpillars and pyrethrin as a short-lived broad-spectrum product. Keep in mind any broad-spectrum insecticide will also kill some beneficial insects, which is why I try to restrict any use of insecticides to the worst situations.

Research on amaranth insects
By far the most research on amaranth insects was done by Richard Wilson with the USDA-ARS Plant Introduction Station based at Iowa State University before he retired. Some of his research papers are listed in the bibliography at the end of the book. He wrote in detail on the lygus bugs, but also other insects he observed on amaranth. He and his students did controlled cage studies with the lygus bug, and found under conditions of high levels of introduced lygus bugs, that amaranth seed weight could be reduced up to 57%. Where the lygus bugs showed up on their own, seed weight was reduced by 28%. These results indicate there may be value for commercial grow

to scout for and possibly spray for this insect, though I don't feel it is needed in home gardening situations.

To look at an alternative method of controlling lygus bugs, one of my graduate students and I did a research trial in the 1990s to interplant alfalfa strips within an amaranth field (Clark et al., 1995). It was based on some prior research that showed that alfalfa, with some portion kept in bloom by mowing alternating strips, could attract lygus. We found that indeed lygus bugs were attracted to the blooming alfalfa plants, but as soon as amaranth started blooming, a fair number of the lygus bugs moved into the amaranth. So that did not prove an effective control method.

Managing diseases in amaranth

The most vulnerable stage for amaranth from diseases is the seedling stage. In the case of disease, its most often "damping off" that causes newly emerged seedlings to completely die, typically under cool, wet conditions. A number of fungi can cause damping off, including *Aphanomyces, Fusarium, Pythium,* and *Rhizoctonia.* There are no labeled fungicide treatments for amaranth, so the best that can be done is to avoid cool, wet planting conditions. Dr. Charlie Block, a plant pathologist with USDA-ARS in Iowa, also has suggested avoiding excess use of nitrogen fertilizer and believes that high seeding rates can increase the incidence of damping off under cool, wet conditions.

In evaluating amaranth for diseases that can occur later in the growing season in the Midwestern U.S., Dr. Block identified there are a few other diseases that sometimes occur on amaranth. In Iowa, he noted that a crown and root rot disease complex occurred where amaranth weevil was observed, basically a situation of fungi getting established after the insect caused tunneling damage in the stem/root areas. He noted that another researcher had reported on Pythium-caused stem cankers, which I've seen periodically but seldom observed to be a serious problem.

Dr. Block also has reported that researchers in tropical growing areas for amaranth, such as Nigeria and India, have observed a serious fungal rot problem in amaranth caused by the fungus *Choanephora cucurbitarum*. He did not feel this disease was likely to be an issue in the U.S.

In my personal experience, other than damping off (which has caused me to need to replant a couple of times over the years), I've never seen major disease problems in my fields or garden plots. This isn't to say that disease won't be a problem, but by waiting to plant until the soil is warm (late May or early June in my area), avoiding excessively wet fields, and practicing good crop rotation, most disease issues can probably be avoided.

CHAPTER 12
HARVESTING AND STORING
AMARANTH SEED

Grain amaranth is harvested in mid-to-late fall, sometimes after a frost and sometimes before, depending on the region and growth stage of the crop. Timely harvesting is important, because currently available varieties have a tendency to drop their seed to the ground if left in the field for too long. This process of seed loss is called "seed shatter" and is a common trait of seed-producing plants that have not gone through extensive modern breeding to adapt them to mechanical harvesting. According to David Brenner with the Plant Introduction Station in Ames, Iowa, there is potential to develop varieties of amaranth that don't have seed shatter, but none are commercially available at this time.

This chapter will address harvesting of grain amaranth first by hand, and then the mechanical harvesting approach used on larger fields in the U.S. Although this book is mainly focused on grain amaranth harvested for seed, vegetable types of amaranths have their leaves harvested while the plants are still green. In some cases, individual leaves are picked while the plant continues to grow, and in other cases the whole plant is harvested.

Timing of harvest

Proper timing of harvest is important with grain amaranth. If you live in an area with a short growing season (e.g., Northern U.S.) or have planted the crop later than usual, you will most likely be harvesting amaranth after a frost. The proper harvest timing after a frost is to collect the seed about 3-6 days after the frost. If you go out to harvest it the first two days after a frost, the seed head will be soggy because the freezing process will have destroyed plant cell walls and caused all the cell fluids to leak out. Allow for a few days of drying to avoid this. If it rains right after a frost, you might have to wait more than a few days. However, if you wait too long after a frost to harvest, the seed will start to fall to the ground, especially during high winds or heavy rains.

In Missouri, most years I am able to harvest amaranth before a frost. There are two visual cues I use to decide when to harvest if a frost has not yet occurred but the plants are ready. The easier one is to simply look at the plant and see if most of the leaves have dropped off. The timing of leaf drop can vary a bit by variety. Among the many varieties I have grown, some held their leaves longer than others, but a good rule of thumb is that the seeds will be ready or close to being ready to harvest right after the leaves have dropped off. You may find that a few small leaves remain attached at or just below the grain head for a week or more after the other leaves on the plant have dropped off; you can ignore those.

The other visual cue I use is a more subtle one and can vary from season to season. To evaluate the crop by this second cue I shake or rub a portion of a couple of seed heads onto my palm to collect a few dozen seeds. When the crop is ready to harvest, the majority of seeds should have an opaque or whitish appearance (see photo below). From my research, I believe that seeds which are less mature, at least among the cultivated grain amaranths, will have a more translucent or glossy tan appearance in bright light. In researching this I found that the translucent seeds had lower weight and a much lower germination percentage than opaque ones, indicating those translucent seeds are not yet mature. It's important to note, however, that rarely do all the seeds end up having the opaque look at harvest time, and it may be possible that the translucent appearance may be tied to genetics as well as maturity.

To keep things simple, you can just follow what's happening with leaf fall. Just be aware if you planted late or have a short growing season, the leaves probably won't fall off until after frost, in which case you need to pay attention to what's happening with night time temperatures and whether a frost has occurred. If you go out one day and, all of a sudden, the leaves have gone limp and are hanging straight down compared to the day before, you can be sure you had a frost the previous night or two, and you should plan to harvest a few days later.

"Translucent" (less developed) amaranth seeds

"Opaque" (more mature) amaranth seeds

Top row of seeds are glossy or translucent in appearance. Some data indicates this is associated with the seed being less mature, although there is some debate about this.

Harvesting grain amaranth by hand

If you want to grow a small patch of amaranth in your garden, it's feasible to harvest and thresh the seed by hand. Assuming you are not concerned about getting a high percentage of the seed, it can even be done in a time-efficient fashion, but the more you want to maximize the percent of seed collected, the longer it will take. I have harvested amaranth by hand many times and outline my preferred approach below.

First, you'll need a good sized bucket (I prefer a 5-gallon plastic bucket) and hand pruners to cut the heads off. Any hand pruners designed for trimming trees or bushes will work. I also recommend a pair of leather gloves because mature amaranth seed heads can be a little prickly; nothing like the thorns on a rose bush, but there are tiny little floral parts in the seed head that can stick in your skin and be a bit irritating. On the plus side, when the amaranth heads are in the early flowering stage, I have found I can handle them without gloves because the little "prickles" are less stiff at that stage.

You also need to have a work plan for where to store what you are harvesting. It's good to have some dry space in a garage, shed, or barn to store the seed, or possibly entire seed heads if you are going to just cut them off and process them later.

If you are satisfied to just harvest a modest portion of the seeds, say half of them, I recommend cutting the heads with pruners one at a time, focusing on the bigger heads. After cutting each head with about 6-8 inches (15-20 cm) of stem below the bottom of the head (that section of stem gives you something to hold onto), hold it upside down inside the bucket and bang it against the inside of the bucket a few times. This will knock some of the seed loose, then you can discard the rest of the seed head. To make the process go quickly, try to avoid knocking an excessive amount of non-seed parts of the amaranth head into the bucket, or you will have a lot more threshing to do.

With a little trial and error, you can get some seed that will only need a modest amount of threshing. For this time-efficient approach, you can either thresh it immediately or periodically take the bucket and dump the contents onto a tarp or wagon in a garage or shed, spreading it out so that it's in a layer not more than 1/2 inch deep (1.3 cm). That way the seed will continue drying and you'll avoid spoilage.

Whether you thresh the seed the same day you harvest or days later, you'll need something to screen out the non-seed parts. I use screens of two sizes, one with about 3/16-1/4 inch openings to catch the bigger seed head parts and stem pieces, and then below it a finer screen size of roughly 1/8 inch (3 mm) openings that still lets the amaranth pass but catches additional small parts. Ideally, you'd have a third screen with openings smaller than the amaranth seed, that can be used to capture the amaranth seed but let other fine material through. However, that slows down the process, so I don't normally use that third screen. I deal with the fines by using the age-old winnowing technique, described below. When screening the seed, you'll want to do it over a tub or plastic box of some type to catch the seed as it passes through.

Winnowing grain has been done by humans for millennia with a variety of seed crops. In simplest terms, it's the process of letting wind carry off fine plant particles and dirt while the seed falls down from one container to another. For some grains, people toss the seed repeatedly in the air, catching it in a container while the wind gradually blows away the non-seed material with each toss. I don't do that with amaranth because the seed is light enough and small enough that it's hard to control against the wind. After screening out most of the larger non-seed plant parts, I take the partially cleaned seed and pour it from one plastic container into another one. I try to do it when the wind is blowing moderately and steadily. If you don't have any wind to work with, set up a fan. Winnowing is a bit time consuming. You can't pour the seed in the wind just once and expect it to be clean. With amaranth, depending on the amount of wind and the amount of amaranth I'm trying to winnow at one time, I find its best to pour it back and forth between containers 7-10 times, each time getting progressively more chaff and fines out of the seed. Even then, there will usually still be a small amount of non-seed material in with the seed. The cleaner you get the seed, the longer it will store, because those other non-seed materials are typically where mold starts.

After I winnow the grain, if I haven't already let the seed dry for several days, I will leave it open in a container for a couple of weeks, again with only a shallow layer of an inch or less so it can continue to dry. If it's already well-dried, you can go ahead and close up the container.

Maximizing seed harvest by hand

If you've got a small patch of plants and really want to get as many seeds as possible (I often do), then you should take a somewhat different approach to hand harvesting from what is described above. Most of the steps are the same, except instead of banging the seeds heads inside the bucket, I rub each seed head between gloved hands to try to get a higher percentage of seeds to fall out. You'll want leather gloves instead of cloth, or the prickles in the seed head will work their way through the cloth and irritate your skin. I try to be quick about this process, rubbing each seed head for only a few seconds before moving onto the next one.

Sometimes, I do this step out in the amaranth patch and then either thresh and winnow the grain right away or lay it on a tarp or wagon to dry further as described above. More often, I'm in a rush to get it harvested, so I cut all the heads in rapid order, tossing them in a tub or wagon, and then haul them into my garage where I lay them out in single layer so the heads can dry further until I get around to threshing them. Of course, this takes up some space and you'll probably be hauling some insects into your garage, some of which will continue to eat seeds, but for me that's not a big concern. The insects either disappear when it gets cold, or I get rid of them in the threshing process. Just be sure not to stack the freshly harvested seed heads in a deep layer, because without good air circulation they will certainly mildew and some or all of the seed will go bad.

To give an idea of the labor involved, if I'm harvesting a 100-square-foot patch of amaranth (roughly 10 square meters), I can cut and haul the heads into my garage in about 20-30 minutes. If I want to do the simple process of getting a small amount

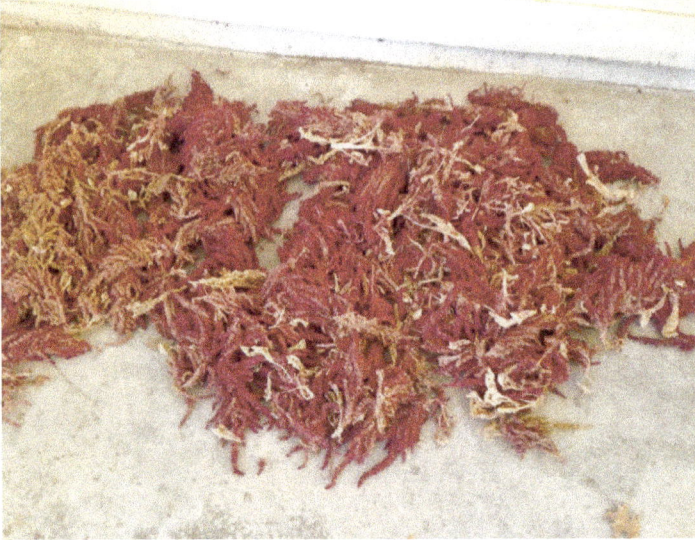

Grain amaranth seed heads cut by hand and brought into a garage to dry before threshing.

Grain amaranth being combined after frost.

of seed quickly and minimize post-harvest time by banging the seed heads inside a bucket and then doing simple screening and winnowing, I can complete the entire process in about 90 minutes. If I do the more thorough process where I'm rubbing or crumbling each head between gloved hands, then I'm usually looking at 3-4 hours total for the 100-square-foot patch — obviously, you would not want to do an acre of amaranth that way!

For my efforts with a 100 square foot area, I can typically expect 1 to 2 pounds (0.45 to 0.9 kg) of cleaned seed, not a lot but enough to use for a few recipes.

There are mechanical small-scale threshers available to work with a variety of crops. I haven't tried any with amaranth, but a system incorporating a small mechanical thresher could probably work to harvest an acre of amaranth, cutting the heads off by hand but then using the mechanical thresher to process the heads more quickly. Realistically, growing anything over 1000 square feet of amaranth will necessitate mechanizing at least part of the harvesting process if only a single person is doing the harvesting.

Mechanical harvesting of grain amaranth fields

I have harvested grain amaranth several years with small self-propelled "plot" combines, and assisted a few farmers with using larger traditional combines to harvest amaranth. Because of the small seed size, it's not as straight forward as harvesting wheat or soybeans, though the overall process is basically the same. In fact, the exact same combine harvester used for wheat or soybeans can be used for amaranth, but it's necessary to adjust the screen size being used inside the combine's threshing system. A wheat or "all-crop" platform grain head on a combine works well for combining amaranth. Usually the header is run 2-3 feet off the ground, depending on the height of the amaranth. It's best to minimize the amount of stem material going through the combine because it is often higher moisture than the seed head, especially before frost. In fact, I've found I sometimes have to wait a week or two after leaf drop (before frost) to be able to combine due to excess moisture in the stems. However, don't wait too long or the plants will dry out so much that seed shatter will become a problem and seed loss will be high during combining. If all goes well, and you have a good stand of amaranth on good soil, you might harvest 1000 pounds per acre (1100 kilograms per hectare) or more.

Installing the right size of screen in the combine is important for efficient harvest. Although no manufacturer will sell amaranth-specific screens, most have clover screens available and those will work well enough. Be sure to do some careful testing of the screens being used to make sure they will work efficiently. You can get a few seed heads from the field and try shaking some seed and plant material through the screens before installing them in the combine.

For a starting point in preparing a combine for harvest, use recommended settings for wheat or an even smaller-seeded crop like clover, then adjust from there. The sieve and chaffer will likely do best if kept open 1/2 inch (1.3 cm), but you may want to add a 1/8 inch (3 mm) wire mesh to the top of the sieve to help separate the amaranth seed from other plant parts (especially if you are not installing a clover-type screen). Cylinder speed should be relatively low, generally under 450 rpm (look at seed in the combine hopper to see if it is being damaged, and if so, slow the cylinder speed down more). If concave clearance is adjustable, start with a fairly small opening given the small seed size.

Fine-tuning air speed is also important. Because amaranth is a small and light seed, it's easy to blow the seed out the back of the combine with the chaff if the air speed is too high. If the air speed is too low, you'll have excessive foreign material kept with the seed. I recommend taking a tarp or large piece of cardboard to the field to place on the ground under the back of the combine and see how much seed is coming out the back end. Overall, an hour or two of trial and error in getting the optimum combine settings is well worth it with amaranth, or seed loss can be significant.

Grain bin drying and storage

Since amaranth is not a commodity grain and is not handled by American grain elevators, there are no official standards for storage moisture or grain test weight. Experience has shown, however, that clean amaranth seed can be stored for a few days at 11-12% moisture, but if stored long-term should be at 10% or less moisture.

Unfortunately, many farmers combining amaranth for the first time will find they get excessive foreign material in the combine bin. This harvested material needs to be cleaned (scalped) the same day of harvest or seed spoilage can quickly occur from the high moisture plant parts that the combine did not separate from the seed. Or at a minimum, if the foreign material content is not too high, you may need to get it into a bin with a good forced air system. Generally, supplemental heat is not used with drying amaranth, as that can affect its quality for food-grade use.

A 1990s University of Nebraska extension publication on amaranth which I co-authored (it's now out of print but available online[1]) described how Nebraska farmer Phil Sanders had learned to dry down his amaranth seed in storage: "He bought 300 feet of 4-inch slotted [drain] pipe, taped it together and coiled it into a flat spiral. He attached it to an aeration fan to move air through the pipe and piled the grain – which had already been run through a rotary screen and had the chaff blown off – on top of the pipe." Sanders also advised running the air continuously until the desired moisture level was achieved, and not stacking the amaranth grain more than 4-5 feet (1.2-1.5 m) deep.

The key to successful amaranth storage is to get the seed as clean as possible as quickly as possible, and to make sure that any seed to be stored more than a few days is dried down to 10% or less moisture. Keep in mind that the market for grain amaranth is normally for buyers using it as a human food-grade product, and they will have high standards for clean, undamaged seed.

---

1 The "University of Nebraska Amaranth Manual" can be found with an internet search for that title.

CHAPTER 13
LIVESTOCK UTILIZATION
OF AMARANTH

Most of this book has been focused on amaranth for direct consumption by people, but amaranth also has potential to be fed to livestock. While only a modest amount of research has been done on amaranth for livestock, both the grain and the foliage (forage biomass) have shown potential. I'll start with some general discussion of the use of amaranth grain, then look at forage use of amaranth, and then discuss some research results specific to each major livestock species in terms of amaranth use. While the research that's been done to date on this subject has been helpful, there is a great need for more research on how amaranth can best be used with livestock.

Use of amaranth grain for livestock

Amaranth grain is a viable feed for most livestock from the standpoint of nutrition and palatability. However, the fact that amaranth grain normally costs quite a bit more than common feed grains (corn, oats, etc.) makes it somewhat unlikely to be used as a primary feed source. Where it may have value is as a nutritional supplement to livestock feed primarily coming from other sources. For example, amaranth added to a ration of corn can improve the amino acid profile of the feed mix as well as the overall protein content. Other benefits such as somewhat higher fat, iron, zinc and Vitamin A (compared to corn) are of value to most livestock species.

Although I'll cite below some research findings on feeding amaranth to specific livestock species, it's safe to say that considerably more research is needed in this area. Palatability, feed performance, and potential for anti-nutritional factors are areas that could all use some further study, though some of the basics have been evaluated. A few studies over the years have reported that unprocessed amaranth grain fed as a high percentage of the diet caused some reduction in animal weight gain, or other performance characteristics were noted. In some of those cases, heat treatment of various types helped eliminate problems. In other studies, raw amaranth grain was fed with no problem for livestock performance, but most often those studies used a lower percentage of amaranth in the diet.

Use of amaranth forage for livestock

I actually think there is more potential for amaranth to be used as a forage for livestock than simply feeding the grain. I base this in part on the fact there are some amaranth genotypes that are remarkably vigorous and produce a lot of biomass, and can do so under relatively dry conditions. Some of these genotypes grow well over 2 meters tall and are quite leafy. Unfortunately, there is even less research on amaranth as a forage than as a feed grain for livestock. There's also been no real breeding of amaranth varieties specifically for forage use, such as selecting for maximum biomass and good quality forage.

The most in-depth work in the U.S. on amaranth as a forage I am aware of was done by Byron Sleugh, both while he was a faculty member at Western Kentucky University in the early 2000s, and the research he did as part of his Ph.D. studies at Iowa State University in the late 1990s. Sleugh was able to make some headway in identifying better types of amaranth for forage use and evaluating different ways of handling amaranth forage. He also studied feeding amaranth to sheep, as will be detailed in the sheep section below.

In general, Sleugh found that grain amaranths had good forage quality characteristics, with the significant caution that high nitrate levels in the leaves are a potential problem. Time of harvest, level of nitrogen fertilization, weather condition, and variety are all factors that can affect nitrate levels, so more research on this is needed (dry weather and excess N fertilizer make high nitrates in the leaves more likely). Crude protein levels of *A. cruentus* varieties from his research at Iowa State were 22% and 25%. These values are higher than amaranth forage research done at University of Minnesota by Stordahl and colleagues (1999). The Stordahl study reported that amaranth forage had protein levels of 14-18% when harvested at the flower bud stage (when the flower inflorescence just starts to emerge). At that same time point, acid detergent fiber was 30-40%, and neutral detergent fiber was 43-53%. When plants were mature, crude protein went down to 11-13% and fiber values increased. Dry matter yields ranged from 1.25-5 tons per acre.

Some studies have looked at amaranth forage as an ensiled product, and that seems to work reasonably well. Sleugh fed sheep with ensiled amaranth and had success getting the sheep to accept the ensiled amaranth material in their diet. A more recent study by Seguin and colleagues (2013) looked at amaranth both as a fresh cut forage and as an ensiled forage material and concluded both could work reasonably well for ruminant animals (cattle, sheep, goats). In their conclusion, they stated: "This study confirms that amaranth is a suitable forage for ruminant animals. Its chemical composition is comparable, for most variables, to that of other commonly used forage species." They did note that ensiling could help reduce levels of oxalates, which might accumulate in amaranth leaves under certain conditions and potentially have an anti-nutritional effect.

Chickens

A number of studies on feeding amaranth grain to chickens have been done over the years. In the U.S., one of the earliest studies was by Waldroup and colleagues in 1984 at University of Arkansas. They evaluated both raw grain and autoclaved grain and incorporated in broiler chicken diets at 20% and 40% of the feed ration versus a control of no amaranth. They found that a diet of 20% amaranth had no effect on chicken weight gain whether it was autoclaved or not, but there was a slight reduction in feed intake of the 20% amaranth versus the standard corn-soybean meal diet. At 40% amaranth, both the feed intake and rate of weight gain were significantly reduced. Autoclaving lessened the negative impact of the 40% amaranth but did not remove it entirely. A later study by the same research group (Tillman and Waldroup, 1986), found that using extrusion processing for amaranth or adjusting the time length for autoclaving could lead to acceptable results with feeding 40% amaranth in the poultry diet where there was no impact on weight gain.

A more recent study, by Pisarikova and colleagues (2009) from the Veterinary Research Institute in the Czech Republic, tested amaranth as a full replacement for meat and bone meal in broiler diets. They pointed out that use of animal products for chicken diets was being curtailed and many plant-based protein replacement sources were expensive. They concluded that, regardless of whether heat treatment was used or not, there was no difference in weight gain and that "amaranth is a suitable replacement of meat-and- bone meals in the diet for broiler chickens."

Pigs

Given that grain amaranth is a cousin of various "pigweed" species, it's probably no surprise that grain amaranth has been fed successfully to pigs. In China, use of grain amaranth plants as a green chop forage fed fresh to hogs is reportedly somewhat common, or at least was in the 1990s and early 2000s. A 2004 study in the Czech Republic by Zraly and colleagues at the Veterinary Research Institute at Brno looked at feeding amaranth to hogs in replacement of getting protein from meat and bone meal. They tried both dried amaranth forage and amaranth grain (both heat treated by popping and non-heat treated), each as a 10% component of the ration to hogs over a 100-day period. They found the hogs performed as well in terms of weight gain and carcass quality on amaranth as the ones fed meat and bone meal.

Cattle

There have been very few studies on feeding amaranth grain or forage to cattle. One recent study was done by a Ph.D. student, John McMillan, at Purdue University (2011). He compared amaranth forage *(A. hypochondriacus)* to corn, and sorghum sudangrass. He found that amaranth was the most digestible forage, and particularly noted that amaranth forage had twice the phosphorous content compared to corn, which he indicated could be helpful in some rations. A study from Thailand by Chairatan-ayuth (1992), evaluated five different types of amaranth from the *A. cruentus, A. caudatus,* and *A. hypochondriacus* species. The study concluded that "There was no significant difference in daily dry matter intake, milk protein, milk solid-not-fat, and milk production when dairy cows were fed with 37% of amaranth crop residues in roughage."

Sheep

A study by Pond and Lehman (1989) looked at feeding market weight lambs a diet of 25% or 50% amaranth forage *(A. cruentus)* versus a standard diet of 50% alfalfa forage (the amaranth substituted for alfalfa) with the remainder of the diet being a blend of 42% corn and 8% soybean meal. The lambs accepted the amaranth as an alternative to alfalfa, and had no difference in weight gain at either amaranth rate versus the diet with no amaranth.

Goats

I found some anecdotal reports of a few people feeding grain amaranth plants as a forage to goats, but did not come across enough information to be able to recommend it for goats without reservation. If someone wanted to try it, I would advise proceeding cautiously, starting with small amounts and only a few animals before feeding it more widely.

Other animals

The "Amaranth Production Manual," published in 1998 by University of Nebraska, briefly cited some other research on feeding amaranth to a variety of animals. Reportedly, researchers in China found that amaranth could be fed to a variety of animals, not just cows, sheep. and chickens but also ducks, rabbits, fish, and shrimp. As with the other livestock mentioned above, I'd suggest anyone considering feeding amaranth grain or forage to livestock to start out with a very low percentage, such as 5-10% amaranth, and make careful observations on animal acceptance and performance before feeding at higher levels. In theory, the good nutritional characteristics of amaranth should have value for many livestock, but the limited amount of research on this topic makes it hard to make any sweeping conclusions, other than saying more studies are needed!

CHAPTER 14
AMARANTH PROCESSING AND FUTURE USES

In an earlier chapter I shared some of the many ways amaranth is used both in modern commercial food products and in older traditional foods specific to certain cultures. However, there's a great deal more that can be done with amaranth, in part based on refinements in processing but also through greater experimentation and creativity. In this chapter, I address some of current knowledge on amaranth processing and then some future opportunities with amaranth. I want to thank Jonathan and Larry Walters of Nu-World Foods (Naperville, IL) for sharing some insights on amaranth processing with me.

As discussed earlier, the most common use of amaranth in the U.S. and many countries is to grind it into a flour for use in baked goods and other processed foods, such as snack bars and cereals. This is not unlike any number of other grains like wheat, oats, barley, millet, and so on. Although amaranth and quinoa are not technically cereal grains, because they are not grasses, their use is much the same as more well-known cereal crops. Broadleaf crops with seeds used like cereal grains are often called pseudocereals; buckwheat, amaranth, and quinoa all fall in this category.

In general terms, amaranth flour has similar functionality to other common grain flours and can be freely substituted for them in most recipes. The slight exception, as noted earlier in the book, is that a raised loaf of bread cannot be made entirely from amaranth, or any other grain lacking gluten. Fortunately, it's possible to make a raised loaf of bread with up to 50% amaranth mixed with wheat flour. More typical for a home recipe, however, would be three cups of wheat flour for every one cup of amaranth flour. If using 100% amaranth, flat bread products can be made.

144

When you find amaranth in a processed food product today, it is usually because that food manufacturer bought a pre-blended multi-grain ingredient mix from a wholesaler, rather than sourcing the amaranth individually. Why is that important? It means that those food manufacturers have little choice in the type of amaranth flour they are getting or the percent amaranth in the flour mix. For example, a nine-grain flour mix used for a bread product might be something like 85% wheat, 8% oats, 2% barley, 1% rye, 1% triticale, 1% buckwheat, 1% millet, 0.5% quinoa, and 0.5% amaranth. A big reason the amaranth and quinoa are likely to be minimal is that they cost more than any of the other grains I just listed. Certainly, at that low level of inclusion, you're not going to taste the amaranth.

Toasted amaranth flour

An aspect of amaranth flour use that food processors should be aware of is the opportunity to use toasted amaranth flour. Companies such as Nu-World Foods offer toasted amaranth flour in order to improve the taste characteristics of amaranth. This is sometimes done with other grains such as quinoa. It is possible to toast your own amaranth flour by adding it to a stove-top pan at medium-low heat and stirring regularly for six to seven minutes until it becomes a darker gold or light brown; just be careful not to burn it!

Toasted whole seed amaranth and the shelf life of amaranth seeds

Amaranth is sold in many parts of the world as a whole seed as well as pre-ground into flour. Although I'd like to see more research on the subject, it's my impression that amaranth seeds are more shelf stable than some types of seed, certainly better than things like wheat or flax. Dr. Jim Lehman, one of the early amaranth researchers in the U.S., theorized that the way the amaranth endosperm wrapped around the "equator" of the seed created what he called a "circle of life," providing a stable arrangement for keeping the fatty acids (oil) in the endosperm from going rancid, which can be a problem in other grains stored for a multi-month period. However, toasting the amaranth grain (or flour) can be a way to improve the flavor profile and can help maintain the grain's composition.

Pre-gel amaranth flour

Nu-World Foods offers a form of amaranth they refer to as a "pre-gel" amaranth flour. They describe the product: "Our innovative processing results in a pre-swollen starch that enhances speed of hydration, reduces mixing and blending time and can improve suspension." I include this mainly to point out that further research may show a variety of ways that amaranth flours can be prepared. Perhaps further plant breeding can even achieve specialty flours in the way that we have durum wheat, soft red wheat, hard wheat, white wheat, etc. for a variety of particular food uses.

Puffed amaranth

Most grains can be puffed, such as the puffed rice in rice cakes or puffed wheat. Amaranth is no exception, and can be easily puffed. The process of puffing grain involves putting it under high pressure in a sealed container with moisture. The pressure seal is then released, and the moisture inside the seed rapidly expands as a gas, causing the grain to be enlarged. This process of puffing can improve the shelf life and the digestibility of the grain. It can also improve the flavor of the grain, making it more acceptable to a wider variety of consumers. Puffed amaranth is used traditionally in products like alegria in Mexico, a concoction of puffed or popped amaranth mixed with honey and sometimes other ingredients to make the equivalent of a snack bar, sort of like a Rice Krispie treat. I think puffed amaranth has great potential for increased use in future food products. Amaranth krispie bars, anyone?

Puffed amaranth on the left, compared to puffed rice. Photo credit: Ludek Kovar, Wikimedia Commons, license CC-BY-SA

Popped amaranth

Although most grains can be puffed, few of them pop well. Amaranth is a grain that can be popped easily. When a grain truly pops, it "explodes" from the standpoint that the endosperm and possibly other parts of the seed are turned inside out while the majority of the seed is expanding due to the expanding steam inside them caused by heat. Under the puffing process, expansion of the seed occurs in a more controlled fashion. Not unlike popcorn, it's possible to pop amaranth on a hot pan – some people do it without even using oil. However, it's not as easy to toss a piece of popped amaranth in the air and catch it with your mouth as it is with popcorn. The popped amaranth is way too small! Still, there's plenty of opportunity for enterprising food scientists or manufacturers to investigate ways of using popped amaranth. To me, it seems it would make a lot of sense to used puffed or popped amaranth in snack bars to provide some texture, func-

147

tionality, and of course plenty of good nutritional characteristics! Perhaps we'll also see more easy-to-make home recipes incorporating popped amaranth catching on.

Flaked amaranth

All grains can be flaked by going through rollers, sometimes heated and moistened before rolling to achieve a particular type of product and improve the functionality and digestibility of the flaked or rolled product. I am not aware of much use of amaranth flaked by itself, although you can buy "amaranth flake" cereal, which is primarily wheat with some added amaranth flour. I suspect the lack of amaranth flaking is due to the very small size of the seed, and the fact there is not much amaranth in the food market to date. However, I would expect to see more experimentation with flaking of amaranth in the future.

Future food uses of amaranth

What food products will amaranth be used for in a decade or two? There are plenty of possibilities. One only needs to consider how corn is used in thousands of different food products, everything from starches to sweeteners to corn meal, popcorn, corn pops, corn chips, and tortillas, to get just a hint of the wide range of places you could use amaranth as a versatile grain. Of course, the major impediment to such uses is that amaranth currently costs several times what corn costs, and the supply of amaranth is infinitesimally smaller than the supply of corn. Kind of interesting when you consider where this book started, with the Aztecs paying as much annual tribute of amaranth to their emperor as they did in corn!

So far in this chapter I've focused on whole grain processing and forms of amaranth, but just like with corn and other grains, amaranth grain can be fractionated and particular constituents used for higher value purposes and products. It may be that the next growth area for amaranth will be in these higher value uses, rather than as a bulk commodity competing with corn or wheat. Some possible high-end uses of amaranth are described below.

Amaranth starches

All grains are comprised more of starch than they are of fats, proteins, or other carbohydrates. Starches are the principal storage tissue in any seed. What can differ among grains is the exact formulation of the starch and its physical characteristics. Only a modest amount of research has been done on amaranth starch, but even that has revealed the exciting fact that amaranth starch is a uniquely small starch, about one-tenth the size of corn starch. Smaller starches are detected differently by our tongues than large starches. For example, in the move to make fat-free or low-fat products, small starch sizes are desired to mimic the smoothness of a fat molecule and trick our tongues into thinking that the potato chip or ice cream we are eating, for example, is higher in fat than it really is. Thus, there may be potential to use amaranth as a fat-substitute in selected food products. There are likely other potential benefits of the amaranth starch yet to be discovered.

Amaranth oil

As described in the chapter on amaranth nutrition, the fat or vegetable oil component of amaranth seed does have some intriguing characteristics. While amaranth is not particularly high in vegetable oil, unlike canola or sunflower (both can be 40% or more oil), it does have about 6-9% oil and that oil is particularly high in squalene compared to other seed oils. Squalene is a valuable 30-carbon compound used for a variety of products. The traditional source of squalene has been marine mammals such as whales or, more recently, sharks, but harvest of these species is considered undesirable and the supply has diminished. The squalene content of amaranth oil varies by variety, but one study from Hong Kong University by researchers He and Corke (2003) cited an average of 4.2% squalene, with some types of amaranth tested having up to 7.3% squalene. Amaranth has the potential to be used as a good source of squalene, but it's my impression that the work to date on amaranth oil for squalene has been more experimental or pilot commercial rather than a major commercial effort. I know one technique that has shown some promise for extracting squalene from amaranth is to use super-critical fluid extraction; more investigation of such approaches is needed.

Nutraceutical uses

With the ongoing interest in "superfoods" such as blueberries, quinoa, elderberry, etc., it's not surprising that people keep look-ing for the next superfood. As mentioned in the earlier chapter on amaranth nutrition, some writers refer to certain foods as having "nutraceutical" properties, meaning that there are partic-ular health benefits beyond simple calories and nutrition that can potentially be derived from eating that food, not unlike taking a particular medicine. The high antioxidant levels of blueberries are a well-established example. Of course, humans have eaten certain foods when they felt the need for something to settle their stomach, help with a cold, or recover from an injury for thousands of years. These plants may have been prescribed by the local healer or herbalist. While we don't know much about the uses of amaranth thousands of years ago, we can study the nutritional profile of amaranth through modern lab testing, and it can be studied in animal trials. I won't repeat here all the infor-mation shared in the chapter on nutrition, but I will point out that going forward, I expect more claims to be made about the health benefits of amaranth. Some of these claims will be based on strong scientific evidence, and some will unfortunately be based on little more than marketing hype (if it follows the path of other rediscovered foods). I'd advise readers to dig deep into the science when researching health claims of various foods; don't just accept the word of a random blogger.

There is some evidence that amaranth has some uniquely valuable constituents that may fall into the nutraceutical category, such as high levels of tocotrienols, which are precursors in the biosynthetic pathway to plants making Vitamin E. Tocotrienols are sold in purified forms as supplements a person can buy over the counter, extracted from a variety of sources.

Vegetable amaranth uses

Dietary use of vegetable amaranth is likely to continue to grow as Western people continue to eat more Asian vegetables and people of all cultures seek out healthy food sources. Where there may be potential beyond just the fresh leaf market is for dried and possibly powdered forms of vegetable amaranth leaves. As with the grain, there is also potential for fractionating the dried forms of the leaves into higher value products. For example, Mary Beth (Wilson) Thanhouser, after getting a Ph.D. in biomedical engineering from Carnegie Mellon University, formed a company called Innovesca in 2012 to look at high protein powders from grain amaranth leaves, with the worthy goal of helping address malnutrition in places like Africa. That particular effort eventually ended after a few years, but it showed there is some promise in the area of dried and concentrated products from amaranth leaves, whether the vegetable or the grain species are used.

Other future uses of amaranth

While most of my focus has been on the food uses of amaranth, both current and prospective, there are of course many potential uses of amaranth beyond human food. I've described earlier the use of amaranth for livestock and pet foods. I've also mentioned that amaranth has shown good promise as a natural source of plant-based dyes, even being tested for tinting solar cells in solar panels to improve their efficiency. I used corn as an example of a food used in an extreme range of food products. Soybeans are the crop I would cite as an example of what is possible for both food and a wide range of non-food products. In the case of soybeans, you can find them used in inks for printing, crayons, solvents, candles, hydraulic fluids, lubricants, and most notably for biodiesel. Amaranth will never be used as a major vegetable oil source in the way that soybeans are, but like any other novel plant, further research will reveal a range of potential products it can be made into. Amaranth is already used in a small way for cosmetics, particularly the oil fraction of the seed. I particularly think the use of amaranth for dyes and the starch from amaranth have significant commercial potential, as might the squalene from the seed oil. I hope that enterprising researchers and entrepreneurs will step up and find additional uses of amaranth going forward.

EPILOGUE

On the need for a diversified crop base in our world

In the United States, close to 90% of the land devoted to row crops is planted to just three crops: corn (maize), soybeans, and wheat. Even worse from a diversification standpoint: roughly one-third of the U.S. fields are planted to a single crop year after year, and at least another third have only a two-crop rotation. This pattern of growing just one or two crops is repeated in many parts of the world, especially where farming is mechanized, from the grain-growing regions of the Ukraine to rice paddies in southeast Asia and to huge soybean farms in South America. To perpetuate these monocrops, we have to pour on more fertilizers and pesticides than is desirable, leading to costs for farmers and problems for our environment.

The lack of diversity in our crop production also leads to problems with soil erosion and soil health. Our soils in many parts of the world have become degraded by a combination of factors, including lack of crop diversity, excessive tillage, and insufficient efforts to protect the soil. For example, in central Missouri where I live, researchers have determined that the typical farm fields have only half the topsoil depth and half the soil organic matter that they did when the fields were first farmed in the 1800s.

Fortunately, an awareness of the need for diversification in cropping systems is starting to build. A well-known farmer/rancher from North Dakota, Gabe Brown, has traveled widely speaking to the "power of diversity" in healing the soil and improving profitability of his farming operation. Gabe grows several different cash crops and also uses a wide array of cover crops to keep living roots in the soil as much of the year as possible, while adding biodiversity. He also incorporates cattle grazing the cover crops, which adds urine, manure, and saliva to the ground, stimulating soil microbial growth. Through this approach, he has significantly raised his soil organic matter, increased the rate of rainfall infiltration (how much of the rain will soak into the soil instead of running off), and reduced his need for fertilizers and pesticides while increasing yield.

Cover crops, which are plants used to protect and improve the soil when cash crops are not growing, are increasingly being used by farmers to add biodiversity and improve soil health. Cover crops can be legumes such as clovers and vetches, mustard-family (Brassicaceae) plants like radish, turnips, or rapeseed, or grasses like rye, triticale, oats, or millets. Some of these cover crops can be used effectively with alternative cash crops like amaranth, as discussed in this book's chapter on planting amaranth. It is my hope that the increasing adoption of cover crops will help address the lack of biodiversity in many farming regions.

However, we shouldn't rely on cover crops alone to improve the biodiversity of farming systems. Adding a second or third cash crop to farms that would otherwise be dependent on a sole crop like wheat or cotton, or a two-crop rotation like corn and soybeans, can prove beneficial not only for soils and pest management but also yield and risk management. Cash crops often have different optimum planting and harvesting times, and by growing a variety of crops, labor needs on the farm get spread out. Also, the most sensitive time of a given crop to weather may differ from one crop to the next, so if there is a hot dry period in July but not August, that will affect corn more than soybeans or amaranth.

Speaking of weather makes me also think of climate change, which will have major impacts on food production in the future. While a few farming areas may benefit from certain aspects of climate change, most will not, and our ability to adapt to more extreme weather conditions, with bigger rainfall events, stronger winds, larger hail, more extended droughts, and more unpredictable freezes and heat waves will make farming all the more challenging. These tough weather conditions mean we will need to improve the resiliency of our soils and our farming systems as a whole. One way to do that is to have a wider range of crops we can use to best fit particular weather patterns.

Amaranth's ability to tolerate droughts and wide geographic adaptability make it well worth investing in as a nutritious food resource for our future. The fact that it requires relatively few inputs to grow means that it is less likely to have environmental complications and is less expensive to produce. Of course, farmers must have a market for amaranth and an ability to make a little money growing it, or they won't bother adding it to their farming operation. That's why the development costs for amaranth and other alternative crops need to be addressed by a combination of private and public sector partners.

The hurdles to increasing the adoption and use of amaranth are not complex and they certainly can be surmounted. It will just take a few passionate people working with others to speed up the action on amaranth, and gradually, just as with expansion of many crops, wider amaranth use can happen. We only need to look to the past to know what is possible for the future. Soybeans were but a curiosity in the U.S., occasionally used as forage up until the 1910s when they started to be used more as a crop harvested for seed. However, there was little processing available for soybeans until 1922, when A.E. Staley opened the first major soybean processing facility, which was where he had a corn refining business in Decatur, IL. He was significantly helped in this effort by University of Illinois professors and other early supporters of soybeans. Now they are the second largest crop in the U.S. and the most important oilseed worldwide, while Decatur, IL, 20 miles from the farm I grew up on, is called the soybean capitol of the world!

Likewise, canola had no history of being grown in North America until the Canadian government and a number of researchers made a determined effort to develop the crop for their region.

Another example is sunflowers, used by Native Americans but unknown elsewhere in the world until Russian researchers put significant effort into improving sunflowers, leading to it spreading not only through Russia and Eastern Europe, but also into parts of South America (Argentina in particular). Eventually, sunflowers became a crop on two million acres in its homeland of the U.S. and over 50 million acres (20 million hectares) worldwide!

Here's hoping that some readers of this book take up the challenge of helping advance amaranth and other "minor" crops (quinoa, canola, sunflowers, buckwheat, millets, etc.). Greater use of these crops can help create a more resilient food system for the good of us all. For everyone reading this book, you can do your part by buying some foods that use amaranth or other "ancient grains" – that's a good place to start in bringing amaranth, a crop from the past, into our future!

> *Until one is committed, there is hesitancy, the chance to draw back. Concerning all acts of initiative (and creation), there is one elementary truth, the ignorance of which kills countless ideas and splendid plans: that the moment one definitely commits oneself, then Providence moves too. All sorts of things occur to help one that would never otherwise have occurred. A whole stream of events issues from the decision, raising in one's favor all manner of unforeseen incidents and meetings and material assistance, which no man could have dreamed would have come his way. I learned a deep respect for one of Goethe's couplets: "Whatever you can do, or dream you can do, begin it. Boldness has genius, power, and magic in it. Begin it now."[1]*

---

[1] *The above quotation is often incorrectly attributed to the German playwright Johann Wolfgang von Goethe, but in fact comes from a 1951 book by William Hutchinson Murray entitled "The Scottish Himalayan Expedition." Murray's reference to Goethe is based on a very loose translation or adaptation of a few lines by Goethe in his German-language play "Faust." Nevertheless, it's still a powerful statement!*

AMARANTH RECIPES

Grain amaranth can be used in a wide variety of recipes, and many recipes that include some amaranth flour, popped seed, or whole seed can be quickly found with an internet search. A few examples are also provided here for you to try. Keep in mind you can also adapt some of your existing favorite recipes by adding a little amaranth. If you have a recipe that uses wheat flour or flour from another grain, you can typically substitute amaranth flour on a 1-to-1 basis for a portion of the flour mix. Just keep in mind that amaranth does not contain gluten, so you can't make a raised loaf of bread from 100% amaranth flour. If you are on a gluten-free diet, you can certainly include amaranth as a nutritious food source along with other gluten-free grains and protein sources you are using.

The source of each recipe is shown with the recipe. All recipes are reprinted here with permission. Most of the recipes are from Bob's Red Mill, which has many additional recipes using amaranth on their website.

Pressure cooker grains with amaranth

Recipe provided with permission of David Brenner, Ames, IA.

Ingredients
1 cup lentils
2 cups rice
½ cup buckwheat groats
1/3 cup amaranth grain
1 small onion sliced
2 cup parsnips peeled and sliced into ½ inch rounds
4 ½ cups water (should stand about 1 ¼ inch above the dry ingredients)

Substitutes: squash cut into thumb sized pieces, any other starchy root crop, fresh or dried fruit

Suggested seasonings tableside after cooking: vinegar, soy sauce, butter, tahini

Instructions
Please read the manufacturer's instructions for your pressure cooker if you are not already familiar with it.

Place all ingredients in the pressure cooker and secure the lid.
Heat until pressure cooker comes to pressure, set timer for 12 minutes.

As it cooks, lower heat to reduce the chance of charring.
Optional: after releasing pressure a leafy vegetable such as frozen collards can be stirred in to cook in the grains without additional heating. This way you get a green vegetable without using more pans.

Amaranth and flax bread for the bread machine
High fiber, low fat, organic, soy free

Recipe provided with permission of Bob's Red Mill

Ingredients
3-3/4 cups Organic Whole Wheat Flour
1/2 cup Organic Amaranth Flour
1/4 cup Organic Golden Flaxseed Meal
4 Tbsp Vital Wheat Gluten
1-1/2 Tbsp Non-Fat Dry Milk Powder
1 tsp Sea Salt
2 tsp Active Dry Yeast
1-3/4 cups Water
3 Tbsp Honey
1 Tbsp Extra Virgin Olive Oil

Instructions
Make sure all ingredients are at room temperature before starting the bread machine.
Follow your specific machine instructions for adding yeast and the liquid and dry ingredients in the proper order. Set the machine to the basic wheat setting. Turn on machine.

For use in a 2 pound bread machine. Makes 13 slices.

Amaranth pancakes

Gluten free, lactose free, low cal, low fat, low sugar

Recipe provided with permission of Bob's Red Mill

Ingredients
1 Egg beaten
1/4 cup Apple Juice or Milk
1 tsp Oil
1/4 cup Tapioca Flour
3 Tbsp Arrowroot Starch
1/4 cup Organic Amaranth Flour
1/4 tsp Ground Cinnamon
1 tsp Baking Powder
1/8 tsp Sea Salt

Instructions
In a medium bowl, beat egg. Then beat in juice and oil.
Add remaining ingredients to egg mixture one by one, beating after each addition.
Heat griddle to medium high and cook until bubbly; turn and cook until done.

Makes 10 - 3 inch pancakes.

Apple zucchini bran muffins

Gluten free, high fiber, lactose free, low cal, low carb, low fat, low sugar, vegan

Recipe provided with permission of Bob's Red Mill

Ingredients
3/4 cup Organic Amaranth Flour
3/4 cup Oat Bran Cereal or Organic Oat Bran Cereal
1 Tbsp Organic Golden Flaxseeds
1 Tbsp Water
1 tsp Baking Powder
1/2 tsp Baking Soda
1 tsp ground Cinnamon
1/2 tsp Pure Vanilla Extract
1 cup Apple Juice freshly made *
1/2 cup Pulp leftover from apple juice**
1/2 cup Zucchini grated

Instructions
Grind up 1 Tbsp of the flaxseed in a coffee grinder until it becomes a meal. Place ground flaxseed in a bowl and add 1 Tbsp of water and whisk until a gel-like consistency (more water may need to be added). Mix together all dry ingredients and then mix the liquid ingredients, including the flaxmeal mixture, in a separate bowl. Add the liquid mixture to the dry mixture and stir until moist. Gently fold in the grated zucchini.
Line or grease a muffin tin and fill 2/3 - 3/4 full. Bake at 400°F for 16-18 minutes. Yields approximately 8-10 muffins.

Recipe Notes
*You will need a juicer to make your own apple juice. If you don't have one on hand, then you could easily substitute store-bought apple juice, preferably not from concentrate and with no sugar added.

**If you don't juice your own apples, then you can substitute with 1/2 C strained applesauce.

Amaranth carrot cookies

A healthy cookie that tastes like carrot cake. Gluten Free, High Fiber, Lactose Free, Vegan.

Recipe provided with permission of Bob's Red Mill

Ingredients
6 Tbsp Vegetable Oil
1/2 cup Agave Nectar *
6 Tbsp Water
2 cups Organic Amaranth Flour
2/3 cup Arrowroot Starch
1 tsp Baking Soda
1/2 tsp Sea Salt
1 tsp Ground Cinnamon
2 tsp Vanilla Extract
2/3 cup Carrots grated
2/3 cup Raisins

Instructions
Preheat oven to 350°F. Lightly grease a cookie sheet, set aside.
Combine all of the wet ingredients and set aside. In a separate bowl sift flours. Combine dry ingredients and sift again. Add wet ingredients to dry ingredients and mix well. Add raisins and grated carrots.

Use a medium size (1.5 oz) spring action scoop to place batter on greased cookie sheet. Using a scoop will ensure your cookies to bake evenly. Using a fork, spatula or the palm of your hand, flatten the cookies to 1/2-inch thickness.
Bake 12-15 minutes, until cookies are lightly brown. Remove from oven and place on wire rack to cool.

Makes 12 cookies.

Recipe Notes
*Agave syrup was used rather than honey because it's not so sweet. If you use honey you may want to use less than the suggested amount.

BIBLIOGRAPHY

General references on amaranth
Myers, R.L. 1996. Amaranth: New crop opportunity. p. 207-220. In: J. Janick (ed.), Progress in new crops. ASHS Press, Alexandria, VA. (Available as a free download from the Purdue University website.)

National Research Council. 1984. Amaranth: Modern prospects for an ancient crop. Report of an ad hoc committee on technology innovation. Board on Science and Technology for International Development. National Academies Press. Washington, DC. (Available as a free download from the National Academies Press website.)

Sooby, J., R. Myers, D. Baltensperger, D. Brenner, R. Wilson, and C. Block. 1998. Amaranth: Production manual for the Central United States, a guide to growing and marketing. EC 98-151. University of Nebraska. Lincoln, NE. (Available as a free download from the University of Nebraska website.)

Citations and chapter specific references are below. Works specifically cited in a chapter are marked with an asterisk. Other literature sources relevant to the chapter are provided for further background information.

Chapter 2
Alvarez-Jubete, L. E.K. Arendt, and E. Gallagher. 2009. Nutritive value and chemical composition of pseudocereals a gluten-free ingredients. *International Journal of Food Sciences and Nutrition.* 60:240-257.

Asao, M. and K. Watanabe. 2010. Functional and bioactive properties of quinoa and amaranth. *Food Science and Technology Research.* 16:163-168.

Bejosano, F.P. and H. Corke. 1998. Protein quality evaluation of

Amaranthus wholemeal flours and protein concentrates. *Journal of the Science of Food and Agriculture.* 76:100-106.

Bejosano, F.P. and H. Corke. 1998. Effect of *Amaranthus* and buckwheat proteins on wheat dough properties and noodle quality. *Cereal Chemistry.* 76:171-176.

Breene, W.M. 1991. Food uses of grain amaranth. *Cereal Food World.* 36:426-430.

Bressani, R. 1994. Composition and nutritional properties of amaranth. In: Parades-Lopez, O., editor. *Amaranth biology, chemistry, and technology.* Boca Raton, Fl. CRS Press. p. 185-206.

Bressani, R. 2003. Amaranth. In: Caballero, B., editor. *Encyclopedia of food sciences and nutrition.* Oxford, UK. Elsevier Academic Press. p. 66-173.

Bressani, R., J.M. Gonzalez, J. Zuniga, M. Breuner, and L.G. Elias. 1987. Yield, selected chemical composition and nutritive value of 14 selections of amaranth grain representing four species. *Journal of the Science of Food and Agriculture.* 38:347-356.

Bressani, R., A. Sanchez-Marroquin, and E. Morales. 1992. Chemical composition of grain amaranth cultivars and effects of processing on their nutritional quality. *Food Reviews International.* 8:23-49.

Burdin, J.T., W.M. Breene, and D.H. Putnam. 1996. Some composition properties of seeds and oils of eight Amaranthus species. *Journal of American Oil Chemists Society.* 73:475-481.

Caselato-Sousa, V.M. and J. Amaya-Farfan. 2012. State of knowledge on amaranth grain: a comprehensive review. *Journal of Food Science.* 77:93-104.

Danz, R.A., and J.R. Lupton. 1992. Physiological effects of dietary amaranth *(A. cruentus)* on rats. *Cereal Food World* 37:489-494.

Kauer, S., N. Singh, and J.C. Rana. 2010. *Amaranthus hypochondriacus* and *Amaranthus caudatus* germplasm: characteristics of plants, grains, and flours. *Food Chemistry.* 123:1227-1234.

Lehmann, J.W., D.H. Putnam, and A.A. Qureshi. 1994. Vitamin-E isomers in grain amaranths (*Amaranthus* spp.). Lipids. 29:177-181.

Pedersen, B., L.S. Kalinowski, and B.O. Eggum. 1987. The nutritive value of amaranth grain *(Amaranthus caudatus). Plant Foods for Human Nutrition.* 36:309-324.

Teutonico, R.A. and D. Knorr. 1985. Amaranth: composition, properties, and applications of a rediscovered food crop. *Food Technology.* 39:49-61.

Venskutonis, P.R. and P. Kraujalis. 2013. Nutritional components of amaranth seeds and vegetables: a review on composition, properties, and uses. *Comprehensive Reviews in Food Science and Food Safety.* 12:381-412.*

Chapter 3
Godibo, D.J., S.T. Anshebo, and T.Y. Anshebo. 2015. Dye sensitized solar cells using natural pigments from five plants and quasi-solid state electrolyte. *Journal of the Brazilian Chemical Society.* 26:92-101.*

Chapter 5
Brenner, D.M., D.D. Baltensperger, P.A. Kulakow, J.W. Lehmann, R.L. Myers, M.M. Slabbert, and B.B. Sleugh. 2000. Genetic resources and breeding of *Amaranthus. Plant Breeding Reviews.* 19:227-285.

Espitia, E. 1992 Ameranth germplasm development and agronomic studies in Mexico. *Food Reviews International.* 8:71-86.

Chapter 7
Gupta, V.K. and D. Thimba. 1992. Grain amaranth - a promising crop for marginal areas of Kenya. *Food Reviews International.* 8:51-69.

Mlakar, S.G., M. Turinek, M. Jakop, M. Bavec, and F. Bazvec. 2010. Grain amaranth as an alternative and perspective crop in temperate climate. *Revija za geografijo (Joural for Geography).* 5:135-145.

National Research Council. 1984. Amaranth: Modern prospects for an ancient crop. Report of an ad hoc committee on technology innovation. Board on Science and Technology for International Development. National Academies Press. Washington, DC.

Chapter 9
Clark, K.M., and R.L. Myers. 1994. Yield response in intercropping of pearl millet, amaranth, cowpea, soybean, and guar. *Agronomy Journal.* 86:1097-1102.

Myers, R.L, and D.A. Putnam. 1988. Growing grain amaranth as a specialty crop. Minnesota Extension Service Fact Sheet. AG-FS-3458. University of Minnesota, St. Paul, MN.

Chapter 10
Myers, R.L. 1998. Nitrogen fertilizer effect on grain amaranth. *Agronomy Journal.* 90:597-602.*

Chapter 11
Clark, K.M., W.C. Bailey, and R.L. Myers. 1995. Alfalfa as a companion crop for control of *Lygus lineolaris* in amaranth. *Journal of Kansas Entomological Society.* 68:143-148.*

166

Olson, D.L. and R.L. Wilson. 1990. Tarnished plant bug (Hemiptera: Miridae) effect on seed weight of grain amaranth. *Journal of Economic Entomology.* 83:2443-2447.

Wilson, R.L. 1989. Studies of insects feeding on grain amaranth in the Midwest. *Journal of Kansas Entomological Society.* 62:440-448.

Wilson, R.L. and D.L. Olson. 1990. Tarnished plant bug, *Lygus lineolaris* (Hemiptera: Miridae) oviposition site preference on three growth stages of a grain amaranth, *Amaranthus cruentus* L. *Journal of Kansas Entomological Society.* 63:88-91.

Chapter 13
Abbasi, D., Y. Rouzbehan, and J. Rezaie. 2012. Effect of harvest date and nitrogen fertilization on the nutritive value of amaranth forage *(Amaranthus hypochondriacus). Animal Feed Science Technology.* 171:6-13.

Chairatanayuth, P. 2009. Inclusion of amaranth crop residues in diet for cattle. *Food Reviews International.* 8:159-164.*

McMillan, J. 2011. Evaluation of grain amaranth and quinoa as forage crops to improve the sustainability and profitability of small livestock operations. 2011. Annual Report for NCR-SARE Project GNC10-122. USDA-SARE Reporting System.*

Pisarikova B., Z. Zraly, S. Kracmar, M. Trckova, and I. Herzig. 2005. Nutritive value of amaranth grain (*Amaranthus* L.) in the diets for broiler chickens. *Czech Journal of Animal Science.* 50:568–573.*

Pisarikova, B., Z. Zraly, S. Kracmar, M. Trckova, and I. Herzig. 2006. Use of amaranth (*Amaranthus* L.) in the diets for broiler chickens. *Veterinarni Medicina.* 51:399–407.*

Pond, W.G, J.W. Lehmann, R. Elmore, F. Husby, C.C. Calvert,

C.W. Newman, B. Lewis, R.L. Harrold, and J. Froseth. 1991. Feeding value of raw or heated grain amaranth germplasm. *Animal Feed Science and Technology.* 33:221-236.*

Seguin, P., A.F. Mustafa, D.J. Donnelly, and B. Gélinas. 2013, Chemical composition and ruminal nutrient degradability of fresh and ensiled amaranth forage. *Journal of the Science of Food Agriculture.* 93:3730-3736.*

Sleugh, B.B., K.J. Moore, E.C. Brummer, A.D. Knapp, J. Russell, and L. Gibson. 2001. Forage nutritive value of various amaranth species at different harvest dates. *Crop Science.* 41:466-472.*

Sooby, J., R. Myers, D. Baltensperger, D. Brenner, R. Wilson, and C. Block. 1998. Amaranth: Production manual for the Central United States, a guide to growing and marketing. EC 98-151. University of Nebraska. Lincoln, NE. (Available as a free download from the University of Nebraska website.)*

Stordahl, J., A. DiCostanzo, and C. Sheaffer. 1999. Variety and maturity affect amaranth forage yield and quality. *Journal of Production Agriculture.* 12:249.*

Tillman, P. B. and P.W. Waldroup. 1987. Effects of feeding extruded grain amaranth to laying hens. *Poultry Science.* 66:1697-1701.*

Waldroup, P.W., H.M. Hellwig, D.E. Longer, and C.S. Endres. 1985. The utilization of grain amaranth by broiler chickens. Poultry Science 64:759-762.*

Zraly Z., B. Pisarikova, H. Hudcova, M. Trckova, and I. Herzig. 2004. Effect of feeding amaranth on growth efficiency and health of market pigs. *Acta Veterinaria Brno.* 73:437–444.*

Chapter 14

Gamel, T.H. and J.P.H. Linssen. 2008. Flavor compounds of popped amaranth seeds. *Journal of Food Processing and Preservation.* 32:656-68.

Gamel, T.H., J.P. Linssen, A.S. Mesallam, A.A. Damir, and L.A. Shekib. 2005. Effect of seed treatments on the chemical composition and properties of two amaranth species: starch and protein. *Journal of the Science of Food and Agriculture.* 86:319-327.

Gamel, T.H., J.P. Linssen, A.S. Mesallam, A.A. Damir, and L.A. Shekib. 2006. Seed treatments affect functional and antinutritional properties of amaranth flours. *Journal of the Science of Food and Agriculture.* 86:1095-1102.

Hackman, D. and R.L. Myers 2003. Market opportunities for grain amaranth and buckwheat growers in Missouri. Report to the Federal-State Marketing Improvement Program, U.S. Department of Agriculture. Washington, DC.

He, H.P., H. Corke, J.G. 2003. Supercritical carbon dioxide extraction of oil and squalene from Amaranthus grain. *Journal of Agriculture and Food Chemistry.* 51:7921-7925.

Loubes, M.A. A.N. Calzetta Resio, M.P. Tolaba, and C. Suarez. 2012. Mechanical and thermal characteristics of amaranth starch isolated by acid wet-milling procedure. *LWT Food Science and Technology.* 46:519-524.

Epilogue

Myers, R.L. and M. Fritz. 2004. Diversifying cropping systems. Technical Bulletin, 20 p. USDA-SARE, Washington, DC.

Additional Information on Amaranth

For additional information on amaranth, besides literature cited earlier, I encourage readers to visit the **Amaranth Institute** website at:

www.amaranthinstitute.org

The Amaranth Institute is a non-profit, all volunteer organization that serves to exchange information among people interested in amaranth, particulary development of grain amaranth. The organization organizes a periodic meeting, typically every two years, so that people can share presentations on their work and discuss the latest progress with the crop. Meetings are held in a variety of locations, primarily the U.S., but sometimes in other countries. Most of the biennial meetings or conferences have people from several different countries attending.

The Institute also operates a listserve that anyone with an interest in amaranth can participate in. Questions and comments about amaranth are posted periodically on the listserve. The organization website has a link to join this free listserve.

www.ingramcontent.com/pod-product-compliance
Lightning Source LLC
Chambersburg PA
CBHW041257040426
42334CB00028BA/3056